TRAGEDY AT MONTPELIER

The Untold Story of Ten Confederate Deserters From North Carolina

Jayne E. Blair

HERITAGE BOOKS
2006

HERITAGE BOOKS

AN IMPRINT OF HERITAGE BOOKS, INC.

Books, CDs, and more—Worldwide

For our listing of thousands of titles see our website
at
www.HeritageBooks.com

Published 2006 by
HERITAGE BOOKS, INC.
Publishing Division
65 East Main Street
Westminster, Maryland 21157-5026

International Standard Book Number: 978-0-7884-2370-3

TABLE OF CONTENTS

About the Author

Raised in Buffalo, New York, Jayne E. Blair joined the U.S. Navy upon graduation from high school and was honorably discharged six years later while stationed in Texas. Remaining in Texas, Blair settled in Dallas, where she joined the Dallas Police Department, first as a jail matron and then as an Airport Police Officer. It was while serving as an Airport Officer that she returned to school to receive her Associate Degree from Eastfield College.

Upon graduation, Blair took a month off to travel and found herself in Gettysburg, Pennsylvania, where she became intrigued with the stories told by the guides. Dissatisfied with some of the information purveyed, and at the same time fascinated with the untold tidbits of information gathered along her journey, she decided to spend her time and energy discovering the rest of the story. Upon her retirement after twenty-two years of service, Blair moved to Virginia to pursue her dream and started a quest to chase history.

Blair is currently employed as an interpreter at Montpelier, the home of James Madison, and has served also as an interpreter at Monticello.

Acknowledgements

I am an interpreter at Montpelier and as such receive many questions. One of the most asked question is "What happened here during the Civil War?" To answer this question and to satisfy my own curiosity, I decided to look into the subject. My quest led me first to the Orange County Historical Society located in Orange Virginia. There I ran across a letter in their archives which referred to troops being camped on the grounds, courts-martial being held and made reference to the fact that "several deserters were executed and buried on the grounds." All of this took place on the large plantation that once was the home of President James Madison. When asked for details of the execution, no one could or would shed any light or information on it. My curiosity was picqued and I had to find out for myself if indeed an execution took place. If it did, who was executed and what were the circumstances involved? Why did it happen? To find the answers to those questions became a motivating force and the quest took on a life of its own.

Many calls were made and letters written in seeking information and advice, as I was new at the game of research. Hours were spent on the Internet searching for facts and leads. There were hundreds of hours spent driving to many localities to look through newspaper archives and court records, all in an attempt to learn who was executed. Meetings and discussions were held with local Civil War historians and scholars. Bits and pieces began to emerge and finally the question was answered. An execution did take place on September 5, 1863. On that day, ten men went to their deaths someplace on the grounds of Montpelier. The exact spot has not yet been discovered.

i

The more I learned of this event, the more I shared with my co-workers at Montpelier. Most, if not all, were interested and one shared this information with a visitor from Maryland. He had come seeking information not only on Madison but also looking for information on Confederate regiments that might have camped on or near the home. Upon learning of the execution, he made efforts to contact me. He was deeply interested in the subject and made reference to the Third North Carolina Regiment, suggesting that I look to certain companies within that regiment. That phone call from Milton Duvall renewed my vigor, my desire and my determination to find some personal information on the men who went to their deaths on that September day.

In this quest, many people assisted and gave me the encouragement that a novice like myself needs to complete such a project. My thanks first are extended to Beth Taylor, Educational Director at Montpelier, who always provided a positive atmosphere in which to work and to Lee Langston-Harrison, the Curator and her able assistant Allison Enos who allowed me access to the Montpelier Archives. Thanks also to my fellow employees and interpreters of history at Montpelier, who were always there for me and provided the needed incentive and encouragement to stay with this project when I felt like giving up.

Thanks are also extended to Ruth Coski, Librarian at the Eleanor Brockenbrough Library of the Museum of the Confederacy in Richmond, for her patience, her endurance and her understanding. She took time to search through the papers of General George Steuart, remembering that it was I who kept asking her for information. She discovered a piece of the puzzle that gave me the proof I needed to know I was on the right track.

My appreciation also goes to the clerks and librarians at the National Archives, the Alderman Library at the University of Virginia, the Virginia Historical Society, and the State Archives in Raleigh North Carolina for their patience in teaching this novice how to search their files, records and how to use a microfiche machine.

I want to extend thanks to JoAnn Jackson of the Cumberland Cross Creek Cemetery Association for personally escorting me around Fayetteville. She took time to look up the name of Mallett and was able to locate the grave of Richardson Mallett. She also provided insight into the Mallett family of Fayetteville. Many thanks are also extended also to Jill D. Snider. It was Ms. Snider that spent her time and energy searching through the archives and student records at the University of North Carolina at Chapel Hill for the scholastic records of that young adjutant.

In traveling about and checking with various sources, I discovered that the Civil War is still not over for some and the idea of desertion during that war still casts a repugnant shadow on the participants. When checking with a librarian in North Carolina concerning information on one of the deserters, the individual was very helpful and cooperative until it was learned that the information sought was on a deserter. The smile disappeared as help did also. I was politely informed that "we don't want to hear or know anything of them."

But to the many people who did listen to me over and over again, I want to say thank you from the bottom of my heart for all of your patience. I know that at times it must have been boring to hear the same information over and over again.

iii

My neighbor, Carolyn Amundson, always smiled and expressed her confidence not only in me but also in the project. She was there to listen, to offer words of encouragement and always knew the story would be told.

Last, but not least, how can I forget my family? I want to let them know how much I appreciated them and to say thank you for their support. To my brother and his wife, Ronald and Judy Harris, and my sister, Donna Blair, all I can say is thank you for being there. You were there for me when I needed it the most and never discouraged me. You listened to me and worried when I was out on the road searching for information, especially one time in the midst of a hurricane. All I can say on that is "sorry, " but I had to pursue that one piece of information. Your love and support kept me going when all else was caving in.

And then to those ten men who went to their deaths almost one hundred forty years ago and are lying in an unmarked grave, you are not forgotten. Even though you deserted your comrades in arms and ultimately paid the supreme price for your actions, your existence has not been completely obliterated. I have come to know you as I searched for information on you and feel as if I understand what motivated some of you to take what steps you did. One day when your graves are discovered, your names and existence will finally be acknowledged.

iv

Chapter One

Montpelier

As an interpreter at Montpelier, one of the most frequently asked question I receive is what happened here during the Civil War. Montpelier, the former home of President James Madison and his wife Dolley, sits on a tract of land that is picturesque in every sense of the word, and gives one a sense of beauty, peace and tranquility. But that was not always the case. To appreciate what transpired on the land during the Civil War, it becomes necessary to explain a brief history of the land, its occupants and its importance.

Well, every story has a beginning and this one begins when Ambrose Madison, the president's grandfather, received a patent on land in the Piedmont area of Virginia in the 1720's. Ambrose had married one of the daughters of James Taylor and, as a wedding gift, received the patent. Taylor had come to possess various land grants in the Piedmont area when he, along with Governor Alexander Spotswood and others, all members of Knights of the Golden Horseshoe, explored ways to access Lake Erie from Virginia. Additional land grants were given by the Crown for sponsoring individuals and bringing them into the colonies. *Price to be paid*

In order to receive clear title to the land, Ambrose Madison was required to develop the land and to establish a residence. He left twenty-nine slaves in care of an overseer and returned to King and Queen County where he resumed his businesses. By 1732, the land was ready and the house built. Ambrose then brought his wife Francis and their three children to the home he called Mount Pleasant. Soon after arriving,

Grandfather James Madison.

Ambrose took ill and died August 27, 1732 under what was mysterious circumstances. At the time, it was believed he had been poisoned by three slaves, two of his own and one from an adjourning plantation owned by Joseph Hawkins. All three slaves were tried and convicted. Pompey, the slave from the Hawkins' Plantation, was hung the following day. This was the first recorded execution of a slave in this area of the Piedmont. The two Madison slaves, Turk and a female named Dido, each received twenty-nine lashes at the common whipping post and were returned to Ambrose's widow. There, they remained in her household for the rest of their lives and it is not known how involved they were in their master's death.

Ambrose's widow, Francis, continued to run Mount Pleasant, until her eldest son, James, came of age. He took over supervision of the plantation and, with his mother's wisdom and support, ran a very profitable estate. In 1749, James married Nellie Conway and brought her to the Piedmont area. Their first child, James, Jr., was born on March 16, 1751.

Close to MM As his family grew in numbers, Colonel Madison, as James Madison Senior would later be called, decided to build a home of his own, half a mile from his mother's. Construction was completed in 1760. It was here and at their grandmother's home at Mount Pleasant, the Madison children received their primary education. At the age of eleven, young James was sent off to school and would later attended the University of New Jersey. In 1774, James Junior had his first taste of politics when elected to the Committee of Safety in Orange County and, two years later, became a delegate to the Virginia Convention. This was the start of a life long career of public service that would spanned over four decades.

2

After a long and arduous war to throw off the yoke of British domination, peace was declared in 1781 when a new nation, known as the United States, came into existence. At that time, it was governed by the Articles of Confederation which loosely held the thirteen colonies together in a confederation of states where each state governed its own affairs. Each state maintained its own sovereignty. There were a lot of problems with the Articles and a convention was held in Annapolis in 1786 to see if some of the deficiencies could be corrected. That convention proved to be a failure for only five of the thirteen states sent delegates. But it did lay the groundwork for another convention to be held the following year in Philadelphia. It was at this convention that James Madison, in his mid-thirties, along with other delegates, proposed a new idea for a strong central government. That government would be bicameral and consist of three branches.

Madison, prior to going to both of these conventions, devoted his time to studying various forms of governments and confederations focusing on why they work but paying more attention as to why they failed. A lot of this studying was done at Montpelier. Madison was considered a leading supporter and fighter for the idea of a strong central government, one in which the states would give power to the Federal government and not vice verses. Many of his ideas were ultimately adopted and formed the basis of today's Federal Constitution. According to Robert A. Rutland, a leading authority on James Madison, "Madison stood as the forefront of the Founders who invented a form of government that the world admires and tries to imitate with every sunrise."[1]

By 1790, the newly formed government was ratified

and operational. Madison was elected as a delegate from his home county to the House of Representatives, where he served for the next eight years. While serving in the House in 1794 in Philadelphia, James met a young widow, seventeen years his junior. Dolley Payne Todd had lost her husband and an infant son in a yellow fever epidemic the year before, leaving her to raise her first born son. Four months after being introduced, the Madison's were married.

At the end of his fourth term as a congressman, Madison decided to retire to Montpelier and take charge for the first time of running his father's large plantation. His father was ailing and eventually upon his death, the plantation would be his. Upon returning home, the younger Madison added a four-room addition to his father's house, which would serve as a home to him and his bride. As he tried to concentrate on running the plantation, his mind was always on the nation. He, through the use of his pen and words, became one of the movers and shakers to the idea of a two-party political system.

Upon the urging of his best friend Thomas Jefferson, Madison once again entered the world of politics when he became Jefferson's Secretary of State. In the meantime, Dolley quickly endeared herself to the nation as she assumed the role of the nation's hostess for the next sixteen years, eight years as Jefferson's hostess, for he being a widower, and eight years as her husband's. For her husband followed Jefferson as the nation's leader in 1809 when he assumed the presidency. On March 4, 1809, Madison raised his hand and took the oath of office, the same oath he helped to write.

A second war with Great Britain broke out in 1812 and, two years later, Madison and his cabinet were forced to flee the city as British soldiers entered Washington in late August 1814. As the British soldiers moved towards the President's House, Dolley was credited with saving a very valuable portrait of George Washington painted by Gilbert Stuart. The war was unpopular and some, mainly in the northeast, talked of seceding from the Union and rejoining the British Empire as a British protectorate. Eventually cooler heads did prevailed and peace was declared by the end of the year. Though it was unpopular war, in the long run, it established the independence and sovereignty once and for all of the United States. With the end of the war, Madison's popularity soared as he reunited the various factions of the government and the people. War President Popular.

At the expiration of his second term, Madison and his wife retired from the political scene and returned to their wonderful home in Orange County. There, they continued the graciousness for which they were known. Montpelier received numerous visitors as the door was always open and the welcome mat was always out. Politicians often sought Madison's advice on issues of the day as he was considered a leading authority on the Constitution, and many wondered what was on the mind of the Founding Fathers when they wrote that document. Madison, often referred to as "The Father of the Constitution" by his contemporaries, remained unto his dying days an ardent supporter and defender of a strong national government.

During the early 1830's the idea of secession had been broached and, indeed, considered by many prominent and experienced Southern politicians. Many sought Madison's

5

Madison leading authority. Constitution.

advice on the topic and, when asked in1832 for his thoughts, wrote: "The idea that a Constitution which has been so fruitful of blessings, and a Union admitted to be the only guardian of the peace, liberty and happiness of the people of the States comprising it should be broken up and scattered to the winds without greater than any existing causes is more painful than words can express."[2] A year prior, Madison had written that the whole notion of secession could "quickly kindle the passions which are the forerunners of war."[3]

As Madison's health declined, his mind and thoughts were on this country. He was the last of the "Founding Fathers" and he wanted to leave advice for others to follow. In 1834, he wrote: "It will be entitled therefore to whatever weight can be derived from good intentions, and from the experience of one who has served his country in various stations through a period of forty years, who espoused in his youth and adhered through his life to the cause of its liberty, and who has borne a part in most of the great transactions which will constitute epochs of its destiny. The advice nearest to my heart and deepest in my convictions is that the Union of the States be cherished and perpetuated. Let the open enemy to it be regarded as a Pandora with her box opened."[4]

That Pandora's box was opened twenty-five years after Madison's death when this country experienced a great civil war in the 1860's. That war tore this nation apart — a nation that James Madison and many others strove to establish. Because of financial situations, Dolley was forced to sell the plantation in 1844, eight years after her husband's death. The house and the land, now a little under 1,800 acres, was first sold to Henry W. Moncure (1844-1848). Afterwards, there would be many others who claimed ownership of the land and house known as Montpelier. Benjamin Thornton (1848-1854), William MacFarland (1854-1855), and Alfred V. Scott (1855-1857) owned the land before it was purchased in 1857 by Thomas Carson.

Carson, an Irish immigrant, appears for the first time on the 1850 U.S. Census rolls for the state of Maryland. He was about forty-four years old when he and his wife Ellen purchased the home. It is believed that Thomas had wanted to use Montpelier as his summer residence since his business required his attention in Baltimore where he was reputed to be a "well-known" banker."

The War for Southern Independence, or the War Between the States, erupted on American soil in 1861. The young soldiers were full of vim and vigor and ready for a fight. They had a wonderful cavalier attitude and were ready for anything. Courage and morale were at its highest. That courage would be tested over the next several years as armies of the United States clashed with the newly formed armies of the Confederacy. Men eagerly enlisted to "do their duty," to represent their county, their state. After all the war would not last long. At first it was thought the war would be over quickly but, alas, it was not, and it proved to be a very long drawn-out affair that not only affected the men engaged in actual combat but also the lives of most everyone residing in the country, both North and South.

As the various armies jockeyed for position, Thomas Carson went about his business and often visited his home at Montpelier. Because of some of his activities though, Carson was thought to be a Union sympathizer, for in 1861, he, along with several other businessmen, contributed to a fund that provided firearms to the Baltimore Police after several of the businessmen had been attacked by Confederate loyalists at the outbreak of hostilities.

But as Baltimore was placed under Federal authority, according to a reporter for the Richmond Enquirer visiting Montpelier in August 1863, Thomas Carson "on returning from a visit to his place here back to his home in Baltimore, he was arrested and it is said was compelled to take the oath and to enter the bonds of $10,000 not to come to Virginia during the war." As a result, and according to the deed of July 29, 1862, "for and in consideration of the sum of Forty Thousand Dollars,"[5] Thomas transferred ownership of Montpelier to his brother, Francis. Frank, as he was known, assumed ownership of the property. Eleven years younger than his brother, Frank was considered to be "an eccentric bachelor" whose loyalty appears to have rested with the South.

By the spring of 1862, the fields of Orange County were in use as military camps and often functioned as staging areas for upcoming military offensives as the mountains and rivers provided not only protection but also the necessities needed to house and feed a large army. Clark Mountain, in the northeast section of the county, was often used as a signal station, providing information on Union troop movements in Culpeper County. Running parallel to Clark Mountain was the Rapidan River, which, as the war progressed, became an accepted boundary line between the two opposing forces.

Orange County was of significant importance to the young Confederacy because of the important rail link that existed just a few miles south in Gordonsville. It was here that the Orange and Alexandria Railroad connected the fertile valleys of Virginia to Richmond via the Virginia Central Railroad. With the train depot nearby, the region became a main hospital area in addition to a military supply and depot center. In fact, many a night the residents of Orange, or as it was know then, Orange Court-House, saw the fires from numerous camps scattered over the area for miles around. In a way, it gave them reassurance for the time being, but that would change as the war progressed.

This area was also a place where the young soldiers could strut their stuff, which most were willing to do. The residents of Orange County were proud of the men and boys in gray as the war efforts had not really struck home - yet. Military commanders would often hold full military drills to which the citizens of the community, and especially the ladies, would be invited to attend. The young ladies, as all young ladies are prone to do everywhere, watched and admired the soldiers and were ready to provide not only home cooked meals for the men but also wonderful companionship to them.

Dances and picnics were one way in which the ladies of the community could ease a soldier's burden and boredom of camp life. After all, a soldier would much rather have the company of a young lady rather than a smelly messmate; — that is, except in times of battle, then a soldier doesn't care how bad his messmate smells as he is his support and his comfort as the bullets and dirt fly.

Residents in the area saw their fields laid waste, crops taken, animals killed or confiscated, and fences destroyed. The roads in the area were severely damaged by the vast number of men and wagons tramping through the vicinity. The hundreds of wagons and caissons that traveled through the area tore huge ruts in the roads rendering them impassible. In the rainy seasons, animals, mules and horses, would sometimes get bogged down in the mud and, as ammunition was too valuable, the poor creature would be left trapped in the mire. Many died where they stood as they could not extricate themselves from the thick red oozing mud.

Brief skirmishes occurred in the area surrounding the plantation, but no actual combat took place on the grounds of Montpelier. But that does not mean action or events did not occur on the land. In 1862, members of Pope's 5th New York Cavalry was on a scouting party near Orange Court House when they spotted two Confederate soldiers. After chasing them across the front lawn of Montpelier, they lost sight of them and went on a plundering expedition. In this expedition, "They took about thirty horses, a large number of cattle, and some of the younger negroes with them," reported A.J. Emerson, one of the fleeing soldiers. The Union marauders even went so far as to disrupt a funeral in progress, where "they took all the horses from those that were there, except the one that was drawing the hearse."[6]

Records also indicate that in December of 1863, courts-martial were held at Montpelier in a room believed to have been the main sitting room for Nellie Conway Madison, the mother of the President. These courts-martial were, for the most part, minor infractions of military law and unfortunately no records court could be located.

In addition to the numerous dances and picnics held on the land, the home itself served as headquarters for General Fitzhugh Lee during the winter months of 1863-1864. The Army of Northern Virginia spent the winter season close to

Orange Court House. Ambrose P. Hill had part of his corps camped on the grounds of that luxurious mansion. In January 1864, a formal ball was held at Montpelier by Fitzhugh Lee to honor another cavalry commander, James Ewell Brown Stuart.

As the war dragged on and casualties mounted, soldiers on both sides became discouraged. Numerous letters urged the men to come home as crops needed to be planted, wives longed for the embrace of their husbands and children cried for their fathers. Not only was the country split apart, so was the American family. In the fields, sometimes brothers fought against brothers as one fought for the North, the other for the South. Father fought against son. Immigrants coming to this country for freedom from oppression in their native lands soon found themselves with a musket for companionship as they were quickly enlisted and enrolled in the army. They were thrown into the fray as soldiers and quickly marched off to battle.

The dead, if possible, were quickly buried where they fell and there were times when some men were placed in unmarked graves for their names were not known. Sometimes, if they were known, a friend or a comrade would carve a piece of wood to mark the grave and, when time permitted, send word to the man's family back home as to where he was buried. Unfortunately, there were many times when no message was sent for the man might had died without friends nearby or was unknown by those who found him. In that case he would have been buried in unmarked grave or perhaps buried by the enemy. Many times, a soldier was quickly buried where he fell as the army moved on. No word was sent to the man's family waiting for him at home and those waiting could only surmised what had happened when months passed without a word.

Prisoners of war were taken and, if not pardoned or exchanged, sent off to prison camps to wait the end of the war. Conditions in these prisons were beyond description, especially as the numbers mounted with no relief in sight. The war took a terrible toil on the soldier, but it also took a terrible toil on the citizens of the country.

With the appearance of the soldiers on the scene, Montpelier became a prime tourist attraction. It was known that it had been the home of James Madison, the man many regarded as the prime mover behind the writing and ratification of the U.S. Constitution. Many of the men camped in the area paid a visit to the home and grounds, writing letters describing their visit. Quite a few paid their respects to the family cemetery that contained the graves of James and Dolley Madison.

At that time, the only graves on the plantation were those of the Madison family and, of course the slaves who also lived and worked on the plantation and called it their home. But, before the war was over, the grounds would contain additional graves — the graves of ten soldiers who did not die of disease, nor of wounds received in battle, but of wounds inflicted by members of their own division. This is their story and the story of what transpired on the grounds of that most famous home.

---

[1] Robert A. Rutland, ed. *James Madison And The American Nation: 1751-1836: An Encyclopedia.* (New York, Simon & Schuster, 1994), preface.

[2] Jack N. Rakove, ed. *Madison: Writings.* (New York, Library of America, 1999), p. 859.

[3] ibid., p. 858.

[4] ibid., p. 866.

[5] Montpelier Deed Records, Record Book 46, pp. 169-170, located in the Orange County Clerk's Office, Orange, Virginia.

[6] A.J. Emerson, "A Boy in the Camp of Lee," *Confederate Veteran Magazine,* 24,(1916) pp. 405-6.

Chapter Two

Ready for a fight

As the nation went to war, with brother fighting brother, father against son, soldiers on both sides felt they would emerge victorious from the conflict. They believe they were not only fighting for their state but were fighting for right cause. In a letter home, Private John Futch, Company K, 3d North Carolina Infantry, typified the vast majority of the young soldiers who took up arms, when he told his wife: "I shall try to do my duty like a soldier and put my trust in that God that watches over destinies of man in the battlefield as well as in the more peaceful walks of life. You must not dear Martha grieve for me but remember that the struggle we are engaged in is a noble and a just one and that God is on our side and if he is for us who can be against us."[1]

John Futch was one of thousands who picked up his rifle and went to war. Many of the young men who enlisted had never been more than twenty to thirty miles from their home and were unfamiliar with military and camp life. At first, it was thought that the war would be over quickly, but alas it was not. It would prove to be a very long drawn-out affair that claimed many lives, both on and off the battlefield. It was also a war whose effects linger to this day. The war, know by many names, has become the most studied, the most researched and the most intriguing of all armed conflicts. Even to this day, there are stories to be told.

In the first years of the conflict, men eagerly enlisted to "do their duty." The Army of Northern Virginia saw many victories and, for a time, thought themselves invincible. But as the war dragged on, situations and circumstances change. The lives of two sets of brothers, one from Fayetteville, North Carolina, and the other from Topsail Sound, North Carolina, were affected by events out of their control. Of the four involved, only one would survive the conflict, and this is their story.

The year of 1863 proved to be a disastrous one for the young Confederacy. In May 1863, after the battle of Chancellsorville, General Robert E. Lee revamped his army. The army had grown to the point where direct supervision was needed, as it was becoming unmanageable for the current command structure. With the loss of his Second Corps commander, Thomas "Stonewall" Jackson, Lee decided it was now the time to divide his army into three corps instead of two. Lee made the following selections for commanders: The First Corps would remain under his "old War Horse," James Longstreet; the Second Corps would be commanded by Richard S. Ewell, who had been absent from the army for the previous nine months after losing a leg in the Battle of Second Bull Run; and the Third Corps would be under the command of Ambrose Powell Hill, a man who had a reputation for attacking without orders. Lee had confidence in both Ewell and Hill, although neither had ever led a corps into battle.

In June 1863, Lee left the killing fields of Virginia taking his army northward to the farmlands of Pennsylvania. It was hoped that this invasion would dislodge the Union army from their strong fortifications in the vicinity of the Southern capital of Richmond. For most of the war, the fighting had been on Southern soil with the Virginia countryside being the recipient of the brunt of the devastating blows. Her people had

16

seen their land mutilated by the armed conflict, their food and supplies taken or destroyed, their animals confiscated, and the bodies of dead soldiers left to rot on her fields. Now it was time to take these same terrible effects and move them northward. Many soldiers felt as John Futch did when he wrote: "I am afraid we will have some hard fighting to do before we return to our old camp if we ever do. The army appears are all in motion."[2]

The first of July 1863 found Lee's army near Gettysburg, Pennsylvania where a portion of Hill's corps had run into a contingent of Union troops, setting the stage for a tremendous battle. The Battle of Gettysburg was hard fought over the course of three days, and has been termed the turning point of the war. The casualties of that battle were enormous. Figures continued to rise for months afterwards as deaths due to disease and other causes were attributed to the battle. Upon the conclusion of the fighting, General Lee and his army returned to Virginia in a weakened condition. He had lost a great many men including many of his experienced commanders. Several of his regiments were almost annihilated. His army, low in spirit and moral, still possessed strong confidence in their commander. However, Lee preferred the fields closer to Culpeper to rally and to regroup, he decided to move further southward as he "could find no field in Culpeper offering advantage for battle."[3]

Using the Rappahannock as a shield, Lee fell back across the Rapidan, a tributary of the Rappahannock, and moved into Orange County, where his "engineers report a good line for us to take, about 1 ½ miles from Orange Court-House, in the direction of the Rapidan."[4] In addition, the army would be near the rail depot at Gordonsville and its badly needed medical faculties. A few miles south was Charlottesville with additional medical facilities. In the meantime, Lee's adversary, Union commander General George G. Meade, ordered his cavalry to follow and pursue Lee's army. By late July, the Union cavalry, under the command of Judson Kilpatrick, was indeed encamped on a hill just west of Culpeper.

The Southern Army was drained. The last two campaigns alone saw the loss of approximately 34,000 men in Lee's army killed, wounded or missing.[5] [This figure includes the campaigns of Chancellsorville and Gettysburg, as well as the two engagements of Brandy Station and Winchester.] Troops would have to be replaced and trained, lost and damaged equipment would have to be repaired or replaced. Ammunition was low, as were food and other supplies necessary to wage war. Before the next campaign, the army would have to be rebuilt and made ready for battle.

But more important, this was the time that the men desperately needed to rest and to re-group, both physically and spiritually. Within the last three months, they had participated in two major campaigns, and had made long arduous marches from Chancellsorville, via the Blue Ridge Mountains, to Gettysburg and back. Some made the march barefoot, others suffering from minor illnesses, cramps, and hunger, while still others did it with gapping and painful wounds. They had witnessed man's inhumanity to man while in combat, had seen man's compassion to his fellow man when the guns fell silent, and, had suffered not only the loss of many commanders, but also many friends and, in some cases, family members.

John Futch, 27 years old, was one of many who were touched by loss of family in that battle. Upon urging from his older brother, Charley, John had gone from his home in Topsail Sound, North Carolina to Lillington, in Harnett County to enlist on February 1, 1862. By going to Harnett County, he was able to join his brother in Company K of the 3d North Carolina Infantry Regiment. He would also be with other family relatives who were also assigned to Company K: his uncle Wiley and another family relative, Hanson. All three had joined the service when the company formed in Dogwood Grove in June 1861. John had been unable to join as he had lost his wife early that year, and had a small son to raise by himself. During the year, he had courted Martha Ramsey and, upon his engagement, made plans to join his brother in the war. Before leaving for camp, he married Martha on February 11, 1862, leaving her to care for his son.

In late March 1862, soon after joining the company, John had became ill. By May, he was still sick and was sent home to recuperate. Charley remained with the company in Virginia and constantly wrote his brother urging him to get well and "come back as soon as you can."[6] Later, he informed John that he, along with the company, "have bin [sic] in three of the hardest fight that was ever fought in America,"[7] referring to the battles of Mechanicsville, Gaines Mill and Malvern Hill. Almost as an after thought, he mentioned that "Uncle Wiley Futch got kild [sic] at Maconicksville [sic]." Wiley Futch was killed on June 26, 1862 as he fought in the Battle of Ellison Mills during the Mechanicsville engagement.

John recovered from his illness and returned to the company by late January 1863. He had missed most of the fighting. But, by the end of February, he was again sick and told his wife he hoped to get a discharge. "I am not well. I have not bin [sic] on duty since I have bin [sic] here. I am no beter [sic] than I was at home . . ... I expect to go before the

19

medical board when the captain get back and I hope to be able to maintain a discharge from this army."[8] John, unable to get his discharge, marched out of camp with his company as the regiment moved toward the first major engagement of the year.

That came with the Chancellsorville campaign in May 1863. This battle would be John's first major engagement of his military career. That battle, fought over the course of three days, saw the casualty rate high for both Union and Confederate forces. After the battle, John, quite shaken, wrote to his wife saying "I never san [seen] the like of the dead men in my life."[9] Many soldiers engaged in that conflict came away from the battle feeling the same way: scared and frightened. Many, both dead and dying, had been left on the field while wounded men sought and received medical treatment. While many did received medical treatment, there were others, suffering minor wounds, that had returned to camp where they doctored themselves. Others, suffering from physical and mental exhaustion went about the day to day routine without complaint. Some nursed visible wounds while others were affected internally.

Many soldiers, including the Futch brothers, had lost most of their personal belongings. Blankets, knapsacks and other items often become heavy and cumbersome and sometimes a soldier left them behind as they fought for their vary existence. Many simply threw them away in the heat of battle. A close bond existed between men of a company as most of the companies in the Confederate army were made up of members of the same or neighboring counties.

Company K, of the 3d North Carolina, was no exception, with most of the men coming from the neighboring countries of New Hanover, Harnett, and Wake. It was not uncommon for them to share their food, their blankets, and other personal items with each other. Many in the company could not read or write, and those that could, often volunteered to assist those that could not or were incapacitated. Though both Charley and John could write, they were poor spellers and often their handwriting was illegible. Therefore, their letters home were often written by members of their company. Of course, living in such proximity and closeness with one another, there were squabbles among the men as there are spats in all families. However, when times are hard or when someone needs help or encouragement, the men of the company were always there for one another.

After the battle, John Futch wrote home to his wife reflecting on what he had just experienced. He told her, "I thought that every man would be killed and there would not be enough to tell the tale of the rest. I threw a way my knapsack on the battlefield and everything I had and was glad to get off without anything. I thought I had seen you for the last time but God brought me through saft [safe] and I feel very thankful to him for his kindness toward me. ... I hope we will not have to fight another battle this year and if we do I hope I will not have the pleasure of being in it."[10] By the end of the month, he was terribly homesick, and again wrote her, "I want to see you so bad I don't know what to do I want to come home mity [sic] bad but I see no chance of coming soon."[11]

---

[1] John Futch, Letter to wife, Martha, dated March 9, 1862. Private Collections 507.3B, Courtesy of the North Carolina Office of Archives and History, Division of Historical Resources, Raleigh, North Carolina.

[2] ibid. Letter dated June 6, 1862.

[3] U.S War Department, *The War of the Rebellion" A Compilation of the Official Records of the Union and Confederate Armies 128 volumes,* (Washington D.C., U.S. Government Printing Office, 1880-1901) [later

identified as simply OR], Series I, Vol. XXIX/2, p.624; Clark B. Hall, "Seasons of Change: Winter Encampment of the Army of the Potomac December 1, 1863 – May 4, 1864," *Blue and Gray Magazine,* 8, March 16, 1991, p. 9.

[4] OR, Series III, Vol. XXIX, p. 1073.

[5] William F. Fox, *Regimental Losses in the American Civil War: 1861-1865,* (CD-ROM), Guild Press of Indiana; John W. Busby and David G. Martin, *Regimental Strengths and Losses at Gettysburg,* (New ork, Longstreet House, 1994).

[6] Charley Futch, Letter to his brother John dated July 14, 1862, Private Collections 507.39, State Archives, Raleigh, North Carolina.

[7] ibid.

[8] John Futch, Letter to wife Martha dated February 28, 1863.

[9] ibid., Letter dated May 9, 1863.

[10] ibid.

[11] ibid.

Chapter Three

The Battle for Culp's Hill
July 2, 1863

When the guns sounded at Gettysburg, Pennsylvania, on the first of July, Generals Robert E. Lee and George G. Meade put their armies in motion. Men and equipment were hasten to the surrounding hills and valleys, and by the morning of the next day, the Union force occupied a three mile section of ground south of the city, running from Culp's Hill to the Round Tops. Lee's forces were scattered in a large semi-circle, with a five-mile radius stretching from north of the city westward along Seminary Ridge, with less than a mile separation between the two armies.

Lee's Second Corps, commanded by General Richard Ewell, occupied the area to the north and northeast of the city, having driven Union forces from the area the day before. Ewell's three divisions were in place. General Robert Rode's Division held the right, which included the town of Gettysburg. To Rode's left was Jubal Early's Division, which was positioned on a small rise that stretched east of Gettysburg. Early's men were about a half a mile north of Cemetery Hill where the Union Commander had established his headquarters. Ewell's Third Division, commanded by Edward Johnson, held the Confederate left, approximately a mile northeast of Culp's Hill, which was almost seven hundred yards southeast from where Union soldiers and supplies were gathering on East Cemetery Hill.

Early on the morning of July 2, a portion of the Union's Twelfth Corps was moved to the vicinity of Culp's

23

Hill, where they would be in a position to defend against a possible assault on the Union's right. Brevet Captain Edward N. Whittier, of the 5th Maine Battery, described the area of Culp's Hill as "bold, rough, and densely wooded, rising from the bed of the stream whose tortuous channel skirted its eastern base for nearly three-fourths of a mile until the southern slopes merged in the swamp, rocky and almost impassable, separating Culp's from Wolf's Hill."[1] The eastern slope of the hill was heavily wooded and steep with numerous rocks and boulders jutting from the landscape as also the north face. Though the southern portion of the hill sloped, it too was full of boulders and thick woods.

When General George S. Greene, of the Twelfth Corps, arrived, he placed his brigade facing east, with the 78th New York on the left, followed in a southerly direction by the 60th, the 102nd, and the 149th New York, with the 137th New York holding the extreme right of the line. Greene described his position on Culp's Hill: "Rock Creek running past our front at the distance of 200 to 400 yards. Our position and the front were covered with a heavy growth of timber, free from undergrowth, with large ledges of rock projecting above the surface. These rocks and trees offered good cover for marks-men. The surface was very steep on our left, diminishing to a gentle slope on our right."[2] Lt. Col. John Redington, of the 60th New York, who was in command of the brigade's skirmish detail, led his detail forward as the rest of the brigade assumed their places. The skirmish detail, consisting of seven officers and one hundred seventy (170) men, moved several hundred yards in front of the brigade and dug in.

As the Twelfth Corps was moving to its position, Lee decided he would take the offensive and launch an attack on the Union's left flank. He issued directives to all of his corps commanders. His instructions to Ewell was to have his corps launch an attack "if practical" as soon as he heard Longstreet's guns opened on the Union left. By mid-morning, Ewell's men were on the alert, but he had not coordinated any of his plans with his three division commanders, nor did he issue any written orders. Instead, he suggested that Johnson's division attack Culp's Hill from his left to his right. Following Johnson's advance, Early would move on Cemetery Hill, and, Rode would move west of Gettysburg to be in a position to strike at Cemetery Hill from the northwest, but no timetable was given for any of the attacks.

The men were ready and waited only for the word to be given. The hours of the day passed without the orders ever coming as the men waited, and waited some more. "Greatly did the officers and men marvel," recalled Lieutenant Randolph McKim of Johnson's division, "as morning, noon and afternoon passed in inaction - on our part, not on the enemy's for, as we well know, he was plying axe and pick and shovel in fortifying a position which was already sufficiently formidable."[3]

It would be formidable. For in command on the heights of Culp's Hill was one man who was well qualified to ensure as such. That man was General George Sears Greene. Greene was a graduate of the West Point Military Academy class of 1823, and later served as an instructor of engineering at the Academy. In 1836, he resigned from the military, becoming a civil engineer and played a part in the construction of the Croton Reservoir in Central Park, New York. Upon the outbreak of hostilities in 1861, at the age of 60, he rejoined the service as a brigadier general of volunteers. His men considered him a "grim old fighter," strict in discipline, but displaying a genuine concern for them and their safety. Considered an expert in building field fortifications, he immediately, upon arrival ordered his men to begin construction of breastworks he hoped would protect them.

According to Lieutenant Edwin Merritt, of the 60th New York: "This brigade was on the left of the 12th Corps. Thrown forward at a right angle, on the crest of a hill in front, was a heavy growth of timber, freed from undergrowth, with occasional ledges of rocks. These afforded a good cover for marksmen. The first duty after getting into position, was to intrench, which, by noon of the 2d, was successfully accomplished, having constructed a breastwork of such material as was found convenient, of earth, stone and logs."[4] Captain Lewis R. Stegman, of the 102nd New York, added: "The breastworks were simple, composed of logs, rocks cordwood, fence rails and earth; but they were formable, and when finished there was a feeling of satisfaction among men and officers."[5]

Captain Whittier recalled: "The woods covering the greater portion of this part of our line afforded abundant material for the construction of formidable works of defence, [sic] and during the night of the first and morning of the second, men accustomed to wood craft built log breastworks, felling the trees and blocking them into a close log fence, battening with cord wood from piles near by, and surmounting the whole with 'head-logs' which later proved of inestimable value in the close contact of the contending forces."[6]

Over the course of the next few hours, the men went to work, cutting trees, moving rocks and piling them atop the breastworks. "Some regiments more fortunate than others had picks and spades, and strengthened their works with earth. All along the line, earth, logs, boulders, cord-wood, brush, in fact anything which could be made use of, was taken advantage of to complete the line of defence," continued Whittier. "About ten o'clock on the morning of the second the works were in a great measure complete, although the men employed for the greater part of the day in strengthening the angles, developing salients whenever the ground admitted, and in Greene's Brigade, under the personal supervision of that gallant officer, in constructing a traverse from his right along the crest of a ridge which, nearly at right angles with the main front, ran back toward the Baltimore Pike."[7]

Later, in remembering the breastworks built by members of the brigade, Captain Jesse H. Jones, of the 60th New York, recalled:

> This regiment was largely composed of men
> accustomed to woodcraft, and they fell to work
> to construct log breastworks with accustomed
> heartiness. All instinctively felt that a life and
> death struggle was impending and that every
> help should be used. Culp's Hill was covered with
> woods, so all the material needful was at our
> disposal. Right and left the men felled trees and
> blocked them into a close log fence. Piles of cord
> wood, which lay near, were appropriated. The
> sticks set on end and against the outer face of
> the logs, made excellent battening. All long
> the rest of the line of the corps, (12th) a similar
> defense was constructed. Fortunate regiments,
> which had spades and picks, strengthened their
> works with earth. By ten o'clock it was finished.[8]

By the time the breastworks were finished, some were five feet high in places, and ran at right angles to Greene's position on the right. In addition, where possible, trenches were dug. The men had dug in for the long haul. Merritt summed it up when he said: "This work subsequently proved of great service, as by its assistance a vastly superior force was kept in check."[9]

Longstreet's guns opened on the Union's left sometime between 3 and 4 PM on the afternoon of the second. At first, Ewell only ordered an artillery barrage to be made. Major Joseph White Latimer, the twenty-year-old artillery chief in Johnson's division, placed his six batteries along Benner's Hill, a half-mile northeast of the Culp's Hill. When given the command, Latimer opened upon the Union position. As his shells whistled across Rock Creek, they began to enfilade the lines of both the First and Eleventh Corps. In the meantime, Edward Johnson had his men move to the foot of the mountain near Rock Creek, and had them lay down in the woods.

As the shells struck their targets, Union artillery was hastened to the area to counter the attack. Lieutenant Muhlenberg, in command of the 4th U.S. Artillery, recalled that on account of the terrain, it was difficult to find a place to position his guns: "A vacant space eligible for a battery was found about two hundred yards on the right of the First Corps."[10] At the same time, General John Geary, of Slocum's Twelfth Corps, "ordered a section of Knap's battery and one of Battery K of the Fifth U.S. Artillery . . . to silence the enemy's battery."[11] In addition to the guns being hasten to the area, Lieutenant Colonel John C. Redington, "sent forward about 25 sharpshooters who opened a brisk fire on the cannoneers."[12]

Latimer's position on Benner's Hill was approximately fifty feet lower in elevation than the Union's artillery. He had nothing in the way of protection, as not only the seven guns of the artillery were targeting him, but also the Union sharpshooters. The barrage continued for thirty minutes before one of Latimer's caissons exploded. Seeing the destruction being reaped upon his guns and his men, Latimer pleaded with General Johnson for permission to move the guns to the rear for protection, saying his guns were of the short range variety, and were not having any impact. After two hours of constant firing, the duel was over, as permission was finally granted to withdraw the guns. A few minutes later, Latimer was severely wounded, and his arm was amputated later that evening. He died several days later from infection.

The artillery duel in the vicinity of Benner's Hill drowned out the struggle taking place southward where Longstreet's staunch fighters were assaulting and tearing huge gaps in the Union line. Meade, his position precarious, gave orders to pull from his right to defend his left. Two divisions from the 12th Corps [Rugar and Geary] were pulled from the vicinity of Culp's Hill, and sent to support the Union's position on Cemetery Ridge, where the Union's Third and Fifth Corps were involved in a life or death struggle that threatened to roll up the Union's left flank. Geary, sensing the importance of his position on Culp's Hill, sent two of his three brigades [Candy and Kane], leaving only Greene's brigade to defend the Union right. Greene reported: "The First Division and the First and Second Brigades of the Second Division were ordered from my right, leaving the entrenchments of Kane's Brigade and [Brig.Gen. Alpheus S.] Williams' Division unoccupied on the withdrawal of those troops. I received orders to occupy the whole of the entrenchments previously occupied by the Twelfth Army Corps with my brigade."[13] Greene would have to hold Culp's Hill with only his little brigade of 1,300 men while darkness and the foe crept in.

During the artillery barrage, Johnson's Division waited their turn, as they hugged the ground. They waited patiently for the order they knew would soon come to send them into the fury of hell. While waiting under the trees, many laid upon the ground using the foliage of the woods to protect themselves from the savage artillery fusillade. Jones's Brigade, commanded by Colonel John M. Jones, held the right flank, while Nicholl's Brigade, commanded by Colonel Jesse M. Williams held the center. Holding the left flank of Johnson's Division was the brigade of George H. Steuart.

Steuart's Brigade was aligned as follows: the 3rd North Carolina held the far right with the 1st Maryland Battalion was to its left. The 27th Virginia manned the center while the 23rd and 10th Virginia held the left. The 1st North Carolina was being held as support and assumed a position to the rear of the left wing. Lieutenant Randolph McKim, Steuart's aide-de-camp, recalled that they "were to storm the eastern face of Culp's Hill, a rough and rugged eminence on the southeast of the town, which formed the key to the enemy's right centre."[14]

George Hume Steuart, who graduated from West Point in 1847, commanded Steuart's Brigade. Upon graduation, he was assigned to the cavalry but resigned from the U.S. Army to join the Confederacy in 1861. When the First Maryland Infantry Regiment was formed, Steuart became its lieutenant colonel. The following year, he was promoted to brigadier general, and in 1863, assumed command of a brigade in

30

Johnson's division of Ewell's Second Corps. Steuart was known as a strict and hard taskmaster. McKim recalled "he was a strict disciplinarian, and it was not easy for any breach of his orders to escape his lynx-eyed observation."[15]

Steuart drilled his men daily, three times a day. Early before breakfast was company drill, with regimental drill following breakfast, and late in the afternoon, brigade drill. His men were use to his orders, and many disliked him, but they were also aware that he "looked after the interests of his men, holding every officer, including the surgeon, to the strict performance of his duty."[16] A problem with command had been resolved with the selection of Steuart, a Marylander, as commander of the Virginia/North Carolina brigade. A matter of jealousy had developed between these various regiments, and it was rumored that the Virginians did not want to be commanded by a Carolinian and likewise, the Carolinians did not want to be commanded by a Virginian. "He had some tough elements to deal with in some of his companies," reported McKim, "and when these became unruly, the colonel was severe in his punishments. It was not uncommon in his camp to see two or three men tied up by the thumbs to a cross-pole."[17]

As they hugged the ground during the artillery barrage, Steuart's men suffered little or no injuries as darkness closed in. When the guns fell silent and were withdrawn, orders were given to advance. Aware of the Confederate movement, and especially knowing they were moving in his direction, General Greene, called "Pops" by some of his men, extended his line as far as he could, about a quarter of the way to the abandoned trenches evacuated earlier by Rugar and Geary. There the men gathered logs and brush, and placed them at a right angle to the line.

As Steuart's brigade crossed Rock Creek, his two right regiments became separated from the rest of the brigade. The 3rd North Carolina, commanded by Major William M. Parsley, and the First Maryland Battalion, under the command of Lieutenant Colonel James R. Herbert, veered slightly southward as the terrain followed the creek bed. Steuart ordered the 3rd North Carolina to perform a right wheel hoping to bring them back into line, and as they did, the First Maryland Battalion, followed suit. Thus two wings were now formed in Steuart's Brigade: the right wing held by the North Carolina and Maryland regiment, and the left wing by the Virginians. The men in the right wing were forced to cross Rock Creek where the water was waist-deep. "Finding that he was inclining too far to the left, Steuart moved obliquely to the right, which movement brought the 3rd North Carolina and 1st Maryland face to face with the enemy behind a line of log breastworks, and these two regiments received their full fire at very short range, owning to the darkness, the breastworks could not be seen."[18]

As Steuart's men crossed Rock Creek and charged toward the southern portion of Greene's line, they came under fire from Union skirmishers, who were positioned along the entire length of the brigade's line. According to Captain Jones of the 60th New York, "In a short time the woods were all flecked with the flashes from the muskets of our skirmishers. Down in the hollow there, at the foot of the slope, you could catch a glimpse now and then, by the blaze of the powder, of our brave boys, as they sprang from tree to tree, and sent back defiance to the advancing foe. With desperation they clung to each covering. For half an hour they obstructed the enemy's approach."[19] Johnson's Division was on the move.

"In the dim twilight of these woods, eagerly listening to that combat, lay Greene's brigade, when suddenly orders were received for the column to move by the right flank and to extend and lengthen its line; and while so doing the 78th New York was quickly moved over the works to reinforce the skirmish lines. The first shot of the skirmish force could be heard at the front,"[20] recalled Colonel Lewis R. Stegman, of the 102th New York. As the 78th New York moved forward to assume their new assignment, Greene's men quickly lengthen their line to cover the entire front. In many cases, the second ranks moved forward, and when the move was complete, Greene's men stood in one single line, with the men standing about a foot apart. According to Colonel Stegman, "to cover this distance there was a very thin line, the man being fully a foot apart, in single rank."[21]

Lt. Col. Herbert von Hammerstein, of the 78th New York, took his regiment forward into the woods, as Redington and his skirmish detail were completely outnumbered. But, the advancing Confederate force was full of vim and vigor and received the 78th New York with the same energy and impetus that they had shown to Redington, and drove the skirmishers in. Lt. Col. Hammerstein remembered he "received orders from Brigadier-General Greene to relieve the Twenty-eighth Pennsylvania Volunteers as skirmishers with my regiment. I at once marched the regiment down to the center of our brigade, crossed the breastworks, and deployed my skirmishers, not being able to see the Twenty-eighth Pennsylvania Volunteers, and having no time to look for them, as the enemy was already pressing all the skirmishers back. Our skirmishers came in soon, and, after giving and receiving some severe volleys of musketry, we fell back across the breastworks."[22]

The Confederates were not going to be denied and pressed hard, driving Greene's skirmishers back and were in hot pursuit. Lieutenant Zollinger reported "We soon met the enemy's skirmishers, pressed them rapidly back."[23] At the same time, General Johnson reported his men "had crossed Rock Creek and reached the base of the mountain it was dark, the enemy's skirmishers were driven in and the attack was made with great vigor and spirit."[24]

Greene sent word to his commander advising him of the situation and asking for help. "I sent to [Brig.] General [James S.] Wadsworth, commanding the division of the First Corps on our left, and to [Maj.] General [Oliver O.] Howard, commanding the Eleventh Corps, posted on the left of the First Corps, for assistance, to which they promptly responded,"[25] reported Greene. Orders were given to Wadsworth to send Greene several regiments. He had the 84th New York (14th Brooklyn) and the 147th New York, along with the 6th Wisconsin put in motion toward Culp's Hill. At the same time, General Howard ordered Colonel George von Amsburg to prepare his brigade to move forward. Amsburg's brigade was composed of the 82nd Illinois, 45th New York, 61st Ohio, and the 157th New York. But until they arrived, Greene would have to hold out the best he could.

While they waited, Greene had lengthen his line and prepared for the assault. Colonel David Ireland and his 137th New York held the extreme right of Greene's line. It was to this part of the field that the 3rd North Carolina was headed "up over the creek and into the woods they came with the fierce Confederate battle cry, and then the Union musketry rang along the whole line, deepening as the enemy came in," reported Colonel Stegman. [26]   General Steuart later

34

commented: "The Third North Carolina and First Maryland Battalion, which were now entirely separated from the rest of the brigade advanced up the hill, however, steadily toward the enemy's breastworks, the enemy falling slowly back. Our loss was heavy, the fire being terrific and in part a cross-fire."[27]

Captain Charles P. Horton, Greene's A.A.G., reported "In the gathering gloom of the evening, the line of works held by Greene's brigade could scarcely be distinguished until they were within pistol shot range. The colors were dropped behind the works and the men closely concealed. The rebels advancing to within 10 yards were received by a volley that staggered through it did not stop the advance. The colors were flung out, and with three hearty cheers on our part, the action commenced in earnest."[28]

The 3rd North Carolina and four companies of the 1st Maryland (Companies A, F, D and C) came under an enfilading fire as they neared the Union positions. Several veterans of the 1st Maryland reported they "were ordered to lie down scarcely thirty yards from the enemy's breastworks. An angle in the enemy's works, not 100 yards to our right, exposed us to a severe flank fire. While lying down, we could distinctly see the Federals rise and fire at us from the works in front."[29] The 149th NY, positioned three hundred yards to the left of the 137th, fired into the right flank of the 3d North Carolina, as they made their advancement against the Union line. Seeing the effect that this firing was having on the charging foe, Colonel Ireland ordered the men of the 137th New York to open an oblique fire also into the ranks of the 3d North Carolina. The toll was devastating.

Devastating it was indeed. Company K, of the 3d North Carolina, "charged the enemies entrenchments on the

35

heights,"[30] recalled John Futch, as he along with his older brother, Charley, advanced side by side. As they closed in on the Union line, the company suffered a galling fire, across their entire length. There was no where to hide or escape this onslaught. To load in the open presented a wonderful and desirous target, so most kneeled to load, hoping to present a smaller or insignificant target. Sometimes it work, sometimes it did not.

Charley Futch "was lying down loading at the time," reported John, when "he was wounded on or near the top of his head - it did not pas [sic] through the brain but I think it must have bruised them as he did not speak after he was hit."[31] John immediately dropped his gun, and tended to his brother as shots whizzed about him and the other members of the company. Charley, six years older, had always taken care of John, and had always been a guiding force for him. Charley had been so much of help, not only for his brother, but also for Hanson Futch, another relative, who was but twenty-two years old at the time.

In a letter to his wife, John lamented about the loss of his brother: "I carried him out, he seemed anxious to talk to me, but could not. He lingered till about two o'clock on the 3d when he died. I remained with him from the time he was wounded until he died."[32] John was at a complete loss. "We had a hard fight thare [sic] we lost all of our boys nearly. Thare Charley got kild [sic] and he sufered [sic] a grideal [great deal] from his wound he lived a night and a day after he was woundid." John also advised his wife of her brothers. "Thomas and Robert Ramsey both got woundid and they was left with the yanky but I hope that we will live to come home without a wound for I have seen so many woundid and died ... Never was hurt so in my life - I had rather that it would of

36

bin myself."[33] In his same letter, he mentions that "I am all most sick all the time and half crazy I never wanted to come home so bad in my life."

As John carried his brother to the rear, the assault continued. In the height of the Confederate advance, Colonel Stegman, of the 102nd New York, remembered that: "They fell back demoralized as the besom of death swept down their ranks. They fought with desperation close up to the Union lines, and then went back and down. Another line replaces them, and then another, the crash of the musketry seeming and being in the very faces of the contending forces. Terrible is the havoc in this area and giants seemed contending for the mastery."[34] It was here that Lieutenant Colonel James R. Herbert, of the First Maryland Battalion, fell after being struck three times. The command of the Maryland Battalion devolved to Major William W. Goldsborough, who quickly took charge. "Our battalion had its Lieutenant-Colonel and Adjutant badly wounded, and also lost a number of men,"[35] reported Lieutenant William P. Zollinger of Company A, First Maryland Battalion.

But there was no time to grieve for anyone who had fallen as the Confederates pulled back to regroup before making another try at taking the hill. Captain. Horton recalled: "The enemy meantime had formed anew and advanced again to attack. They succeeded this time in getting up to the works, and some close fighting took place but with the same results as before."[36]

The left wing of Steuart's brigade had the luxury of cover as they advanced on the Union positions. The Virginia regiments were able to get into a position where they could fired on Greene's right flank from three directions. The 10th

Virginia worked its way along a stone wall on the right flank, and opened a devastating fire from the west while the 23rd Virginia assaulted from the south, coming to within twenty paces of the 137th New York's position. The 27th Virginia maintained a steady and well-aimed fire on the front ranks. Colonel Ireland, of the 137th New York, pulled back a portion of his line to form a right angle in the hopes of defending his besieged line. This action though allowed the 1st Maryland to direct their fire into the 137th New York. There was no where to go but to pull back as he was unable to withstand the assault. Ireland pulled back to the trenches that Green had built earlier in the day. Using these trenches, they were able to stop, load and fired into the advancing Southern troops who had pursued them. For the time, the pursuit was checked.

In reflecting on the situation, Captain Jones, of the 60th New York, said, "The enemy worked still further around to our right, entered the breastwork beyond our line, and crumpled up and drove back, a short distance our extreme right regiment."[37] General Meade later commented: "The left of the assaulting columns, met with success. Concealed and sheltered by woods and under cover of night, some of the troops worked their way around to their left until they chanced upon the unoccupied works of Williams's division, which at the point where the attack struck were perpendicular to the general line, This success seriously menaced for a time the integrity of the right flank of the Federal line."[38]

When Greene was informed of the withdrawal of the 137th New York, his most right regiment, he sent word for his support to hurry up. At the same time, he ordered his right to swing about. Meade reported that Greene, "who, handling his small command with great skill, swung his right regiment to the rear, and presenting a firm front prevented them from making any further advance."[39] The Virginians kept up their assault, and in the meantime, with the pressure relieve on the Confederate right; a portion of the First Maryland Battalion was able to move into the breastworks abandoned by the 137th New York.

The support Greene needed finally came at the most opportune time Two regiments from General Alexander S. Webb's brigade, of the 2nd Corps, sent by General Gibbons arrived. One of the regiments was the 71st Pennsylvania led by Colonel Richard Penn Smith. As they arrived, Captain Horton tried desperately to hurry them up. "I rode to the right of our line, directing the colonel to hurry forward and select their position. The regiment, however was very slow in coming up, and again rode back to hurry them up. They finally advanced and went into the trenches giving three loud cheers as they reached them. These cheers were answered by a few scattering shots from the front and from the right front."[40]

By now, Steuart's brigade was once more threatening to take the breastworks. Colonel Smith recalled that Horton had "assur [ed] me that all was safe on either flank."[41] But that was not true for the Confederates were everywhere. After receiving a few shots, Smith decided to pull his men out, much to the dismay of Horton. "The men of the 71st Pennsylvania rose up and retreated in line, apparently without panic or disorder. Riding up to the Colonel, I found that he had ordered the retreat, saying that he would not have his men murdered."[42] Smith had a different opinion, stating, "Arriving at the front, I became engaged with the enemy on the front. At the same time he attacked me on my right and rear. I immediately ordered my command to retire to the road in my rear, when I returned to camp against orders."[43] General Greene was furious when he discovered that the 71st Pennsylvania had

39

withdrew. "This regiment, without being specially attacked, was marched to the rear by its colonel, when an attack upon it was imminently probable, much to the disgust of his men, as reported."[44]

A few regiments of James Wadsworth's First Division of the 1st Corps had by now arrived. They quickly assumed a position where they were able to direct their fire into the advancing foe. With the arrival of fresh and spirited troops, a portion of Steuart's line staggered and pulled back to regroup before they made another go at the entrenched line. Major Goldsborough reported, "the 3rd North Carolina and the 1st Maryland received an enfilading fire from Green's New York Brigade, which was posted in an angle of the works, about three hundred yards to the right. The balance of Steuart's Brigade was on the other side of the ridge, and was not exposed to the fire at all."[45]

Darkness had by now shrouded the entire area, and the only light was that emitted from the muzzle fire. At the base of the hill was Randolph McKim, Steuart's aide-de-camp. He had remained behind with the 1st North Carolina, who had been held in support, should their help be needed. And now it was needed more than ever. McKim, 21 years old, had served as Steuart's aide-de-camp for over a year, and had gained the trust of his chief. He desperately wanted to get into the battle. "The firing in the woods now became very rapid, and volley after volley echoed and re-echoed among the hills. I felt very anxious about our boys in front, and several times urged General Steuart to send the reserve regiment to the support of the remainder of the brigade."[46]

Finally receiving permission, McKim led the way as he directed the 1st North Carolina into the fray and in defense of the brigade's right wing. As they moved up the hill, they saw movement to their front coming in their direction, but because of the darkness could not tell who they were. At the same time, they were receiving fire coming at them from many rifles and this firing was coming from the same direction as the movement to their front. Believing they were under attack, McKim gave the order for the 1st North Carolina to open fire. "Fire on them boys, fire on them!" screamed McKim. Every rifle opened with great vigor and good aim.

What he and the men of the 1st North Carolina did not know at the time was that they were firing into the ranks of their own comrades, the men of the 3rd North Carolina and the 1st Maryland, who were pulling back under fire. "To make matters still worse, the 1st North Carolina, which was marching in reserve, believing they were being fired upon by the enemy, opened fire, by which a number of men in the two right regiments were killed and wounded, "[47] remembered Goldsborough. Seeing what was happening was Major William M. Parsley, whose regiment, the 3d North Carolina was receiving the brunt of this friendly fire, rushed forward yelling "They are our own men."[48] Briefly the firing stopped as the 1st North Carolina rushed forward to assist the wounded, and then once more, resumed their advancement on the hill. In the melee, McKim was struck four times, and fortunately, he was only severely bruised.

"In the meantime, the attack was hotly pressed by the enemy who now appeared in some force in the works,"[49] reported Horton. But by then, three regiments of the 11th Corps (The 61st Ohio, along with the 82nd Illinois and 45th New York, of Schimmelfenning's brigade, under the command of Amsburg) arrived and helped the battered and exhausted men of Greene's brigade. Darkness had settled in, and, both sides were completely wiped out. It was now impossible to differentiate friend from foe. Amsburg's men temporarily relieved the tired and exhausted men of the Twelfth Corps, who had held the hill for the last three hours, and whose members were also low or out of ammunition. "And thus for three hours there was a desperate, relentless warfare The Confederates had discovered the openings upon the right, have turned the right flank of the brigade, the extension thrown out in the Second Brigade works, but the regiment there simply retires to the traverses and still fights on with daring intrepidity. Bullets are now flying from front, right and rear, but with dauntless heroism the brigade fights on, and there comes a lull in the storm. Four desperate charges have been repelled, and not one inch of the original brigade line has been lost,"[50] related Colonel Stegman of the 102nd New York.

The brigades of Williams and Jones, at the same time, had kept up their relentless attacks and three times tried to take the high ground of the hill, and three times they were forced to pull back. Of the three brigades in Johnson's Division, only Steuart's men had been able to achieve some success as a part of the brigade moved into the trenches where they would spend the night, just yards from the Union line. According to General Doubleday, "they were now but a short distance from General Meade's headquarters, and within easy reach of our reserve artillery."[51]

After several hours of severe fighting, a brief lull of hostilities was enjoined as darkness covered the field. Sporadic shots could be heard and the flash of a muzzle seen, and they served only as a reminder that someone was on duty and always on the alert - on both sides. A response would be made and an answer returned. During the night, members of the 3d North Carolina alternated their positions with the First

Maryland Battalion, whose members were safely entrenched in the Union fortifications.   To prevent Union forces from moving on these positions, four companies from the 1st North Carolina were moved to Rock Creek while the rest of the regiment was placed near Sprangler Spring.

In between shots, the cries and the moans of the wounded and the dying left on the field could be heard. They were stuck in no man's land. The quest for water was paramount. The throats of the wounded were parched, and the more one moaned, the more one cried and the more one tried to breathe, the dryer the mouth became, and the more water was needed. A frothy and white foam covered the mouths and noses of the wounded as breathing became more and more labored. Some went on for hours. Others ceased after a while, either because they knew it was useless to continue or else a resignation of the inevitable. Death was a welcome visitor.

But, it was during these morning hours that man's compassion took hold. Many ventured forth into the field of battle to aid and offer help, assistance and comfort to their opponent. The wounded were carried into the other's lines to receive necessary medical treatment. Water was shared or a hand held or a brow wiped as life ebbed from a body. On other sections of the field, soldiers being soldiers, words were exchanged and many rumors abound that some ventured forth to meet with "their enemy" and in between greetings, exchange coffee, tobacco and news.

---

[1] Edward N. Whittier. "The Left Attack (Ewell's) , Gettysburg," *The Gettysburg Papers* ed. Ken Bandy and Florence Freeland, (Dayton, Morningside Bookshop, 1986), pp. 759-60.

[2] OR, Series 1, Vol. XXVII, p. 856.

[3] Randolph McKim, *A Soldier's Recollections: Leaves from the Diary of a Young Confederate,* (New York, Longmans, Green and Co.,

1910) p. 194; Champ Clark, *Gettysburg: The Confederate High Tide,* (New York, Time Life Books, Inc., 1985) p. 114.

[4] New York Monuments Commission for the Battlefield of Gettysburg and Chattanooga: Final Report of the Battle of Gettysburg, 3 Volumes, (Albany, J.B. Lyon Company, 1900) [later identified as NyatGB], Vol. I, p.451

[5] ibid., Vol. III, p. 1013.

[6] Whittier, p. 763.

[7] ibid.

[8] Jesse H. Jones, "The Breastworks at Culp's Hill- Part 1," *Battles and Leaders of the Civil War*, 4 Volumes, (Secaucus, NJ, Castle, n.d.), Vol. III, p. 316.

[9] NyatGB, Vol. I, p.451.

[10] OR, Series I, Vol. XXVII, p. 870.

[11] ibid., p.826.

[12] ibid., p. 863.

[13] ibid., p. 826.

[14] McKim, P. 195.

[15] ibid., p. 40.

[16] ibid.

[17] ibid.

[18] "Steuart's Brigade at Gettysburg, " *The Southern Historical Papers, 52 Volumes,* (CD-ROM), (Carmel, In, Guild Press of Indiana), Vol. II, No. 1, Pg. 107.

[19] Jones, p. 316.

[20] NyatGB, Vol. III, pp. 1013-14.

[21] ibid.

[22] OR, Series I, Vol. XXVII, p.864.

[23] "Steuart's Brigade at Gettysburg," p.107.

[24] Whittier, p.767.

[25] OR, Series I, Vol. XXVII, p.856.

[26] NyatGB, Vol. III, p.1014.

[27] OR, Series 2, Vol. XXVII, p. 510.

[28] David L. Ladd and Audrey Ladd, ed., *Bachelder Papers: Gettysburg In Their Own Words, Reprint* (Dayton, Moringside Bookshop, 1994), Letter of Charles P. Horton dated January 23, 1867, p. 294.

[29] William P. Zollinger, *The Southern Historical Papers,* 52 Volumes, (CD-ROM), (Carmel, In, Guild Press of Indiana) Vol. II, No. 1, p.106.

[30] John Futch, Letter to his wife dated August 6, 1863.

[31] ibid.

[32] ibid.

[33] ibid, Letter dated July 19, 1863.

[34] NyatGB, Vol. III, p. 1014.

[35] Zollinger, p. 105.

[36] Bachelder Papers, p.295.

[37] Jones, p. 316.

[38] George G. Meade, *The Life and Letters of George G. Meade: Gettysburg,* Reprint (York, Pa., Graphic Works, 1998), p. 80.

[39] ibid.

[40] Bachelder Papers, p.295.

[41] OR, Series I, Vol. XXVII, p. 432.

[42] Bachelder Papers, p.295.

[43] OR, Series I, Vol. XXVII, p. 432.

[44] George Greene, "The Breastworks at Culp's Hills – Part 2," *Battles and Leaders of the Civil War,* 4 Volumes, (Secaucus, NY, Castle, n.d.), Vol. III, p.317.

[45] W.W. Goldsborough, *The Maryland Line in the Confederate Army,* (Baltimore, n.p., 1990) p. 104.

[46] McKim, p. 195.

[47] Goldsborough, p. 104.

[48] McKim, p. 196.

[49] Bachelder Papers, p. 295.

[50] NyatGB, Vol. III, p. 1014.

[51] Abner Doubleday, *Chancellsorville and Gettysburg,* (New York, Da Capo Press, 1994) pp 180-1.

Chapter Four

The Battle Continues

During the lull in the action, both sides received support as additional troops were moved to the area. General Geary was bound and determined to take back the positions he had lost to the Confederate advance. "I devoted the rest of the night, after consultation with Major General Slocum and Brigadier General Williams, to such an arrangement of my troops as, by a vigorous attack at daylight, to drive the enemy from the ground they had gained."[1] In the meantime, Johnson knew come daylight the Union forces would endeavor to retake the hill. He petitioned General Ewell for additional manpower to hold what he had captured the night before, and to resume his attack on the Union right flank. Three brigades were immediately put in motion: one from Early's division and two from Rode's division. But before one of Rode's brigades, that of Edward O'Neal, could advance very far, they came under heavy fire from Union troops and were prevented from being of any help to Johnson, and especially to the men of Steuart's Brigade.

Greene's beleaguered troops had received additional supports during the early morning hours, and were prepared for the attack they knew would come from the trenches just a few yards away. Starting at 4:30 AM, before it was light, General Williams ordered the artillery to open on the Confederate positions on Culp's Hill. As the guns roared into action and pounded the area, Johnson had his man lay low as the shells exploded all around them. McKim remarked: "Let it be remembered, too, that while we were pounded for hours by that powerful artillery, we had not a single piece on that hill to

47

make reply. They marveled that we did not return their artillery fire."[2]

An hour later, the Union brigades of Kane and Greene began an earnest effort to take back the area, and advanced upon Confederate positions. According to General Steuart, "The whole command rested from about 11 p. m. till about daylight, [3d], when the enemy opened a terrific fire of artillery and a very heavy fire of musketry upon us, occasioning no loss to the brigade, excepting to the First Maryland Battalion and Third North Carolina, which in part alternated positions behind the breastworks."[3] It was a back and forth fight as neither was able to dislodge the other and neither would give in or give up.

Johnson had ordered Steuart to initiate an attack upon the Union troops and to drive them from the positions they held during the night. Johnson was "confident of their ability to sweep him away and take the whole Union line in reverse."[4] Steuart though strongly disapproved as his men were exhausted, his manpower was minimal and the area to be taken strongly fortified. "There was a double line of entrenchments, one above the other, and each filled with troops,"[5] according to McKim. But orders are orders and have to be obeyed. "What wonder, then, if Steuart was reluctant to lead his men into such a slaughterpen, from which he saw there could be no issue but death and defeat! But though he remonstrated, he gallantly obeyed without delay the orders he received, giving the command, 'Left face,' and afterwards, 'File right.' He made his men leap the breastworks and form in line of battle on the other side at right angles, nearly, to their previous position, galled all the time by a brisk fire from the enemy."[6]

When the order was given, the assault began in earnest. "The compressed lip, the stern brow, the glittering eye, told that those before me would fight to the last,"[7] remembered Lieutenant Zollinger. "In moving to the attack," added McKim, "we were exposed to enfilading fire from the woods on our left flank, besides the double line of fire which we had to face in front, and a battery of artillery posted on a hill to our left rear opened upon us at short range."[8]

Steuart was with the Maryland battalion as it prepared to do as ordered. "When the final order to charge was received, the General remarked, 'it is a slaughter pen.' A gallant captain replied, 'it can't be helped, it is ordered,' placed himself at the head of his company, and was killed instantly, less than fifty yards from the foe. The task was impossible for the little brigade, but it obeyed orders. The loss was fearful, our company losing sixty-two (62) out of ninety-odd in the two days' fighting."[9] William Henry Murray, Captain of Company A, First Maryland Battalion, fell dead as he gallantly led his men in the charge.

"The struggle for the hill now became more and more fierce. The enemy endeavored to drive us out of the works. They attacked us in front and in flank, and opened a terrific cannonading upon us from a battery posted about 500 yards off," relayed Randolph McKim. "On the right and left flank, where our lines were almost perpendicular to the front line, there were no breastworks, and the struggle was very fierce and bloody. . . .The Third North Carolina was on the right, and suffered most heavily during this part of the battle, so that but a handful were left to participate in the final charge."[10] The struggle for control of the trenches and the hill was frightening in the cost of lives as McKim remembered. "The men were mowed down with fearful rapidity, by two lines in front and a force on the left flank, besides an artillery fire from the left rear," recalled McKim. "It was the most fearful fire I ever encountered, and my heart was sickened with the sight of so many gallant men sacrificed. The greatest confusion ensued, regiments were reduced to companies and everything mixed up. It came very near being a rout."[11]

In the same assault that claimed the life of Murray also claimed the life of Major Benjamin W. Leigh, Johnson's Acting Adjutant General. General Greene remembered seeing Leigh fall: "[the major] persisted in riding up to the very front of our lines, pushing his men to an assault on my works, where both horse and rider were killed, pierced simultaneously with several bullets."[12] According to Randolph McKim, "Major Leigh, seeing a group of Confederates in a very, exposed position raise a white flag in order to surrender to the enemy, gallantly rode into their midst to prevent the execution of their purpose. While so engaged he met his death, and my correspondent said that the day after the battle he was found lying on the field still in the saddle, his horse dead with him as if a part of him - horse and rider having been killed at the same moment."[13]

For three hours, the battle seesawed back and forth with hand to hand fighting taking place at certain places. "On they pressed to within about twenty or thirty paces of the works a small but gallant band of heroes daring to attempt what could not be done by flesh and blood,"[14] recalled McKim in reference to the Confederate attack with the 3rd North Carolina holding the right of the line. "The wonder is that the rebels persisted so long in an attempt that in the first half hour must have seemed useless,"[15] wondered General Alpheus Williams. The fight continued until about 10 o'clock as the sun climbed higher and higher in the sky. "As the day wore on, the heat from the fire and smoke of battle, and the scorching of the July sun, became so intense as to be almost past endurance. Men were completely exhausted in the progress of the struggle, and had to be often relieved; but revived by fresh air and a little period of rest, again returned to the front,"[16] reported McKim.

Finally, Steuart, with the threat looming of being annihilated, came to the only conclusion possible at the time - that of pulling back to their original position behind Rock Creek. But to do that would require his men to extricate themselves from their position. The only way this could be accomplished would be a full-blown charge down hill. He passed the word and in some cases, begrudgingly, the soldiers gather themselves up and "obeyed the order to evacuate the intrenchments and retire to the foot of the hill,"[17] reported McKim.

Before receiving the order to pull out, Randolph McKim recalled the awful situation the unit was in.
On the left was a piece of woods, from
which the enemy's sharpshooters opened a
very galling fire, raking our whole line. This
decided the failure of our attempt to storm their
works, for the regiments of the left first halted
(while the right of the line advanced), and
then fell back.... Still we pressed on. General
Steuart, Captain Williamson, and I were all on
the right centre, where were the Second
Maryland [First Maryland Battalion] and eight
men of the Third North Carolina. Oh! it was a
gallant band. We had our sabres drawn,
and were cheering on the men, but there was
little need of it. Their gallantry did not avail,

and their noble blood was spilled in vain.... It
was as if the sickle of Death had passed along
the line and mown down the noblest and the bravest. . .
Friends dropped all around me, and lay writhing on the
ground.[18]

McKim continued his account of the situation. "It was
more than men could endure, and reluctantly they commenced
falling back. Then our task was to prevent a rout, for the
brigade was terribly cut up and the men much demoralized.
Behind some rocks we rallied the scattered regiments and
made a stand. Finally we took our old position behind the
breastworks, supported by Daniel's brigade. Here we lay for
about an hour under the most furious infantry and artillery fire
I have ever experienced, but without much loss."[19]

McKim later remarked that he was impressed with the
actions of the men as they charged down the hill pursued by
members of the 12th Corps. "To rush forward in the fire and
fury of battle does not test a soldier's mettle as it does to
retreat, under such circumstances, in good order. And I point
to that column, after that night and day of battle, after their
terrible losses, after that fatal repulse in the bayonet charge,
their nerves shaken by all that they had endured, — I point to
it marching steadily down that hill of death, while the heroic
Capt. Geo. Williamson and another staff officer, with drawn
swords, walked backward (face to the enemy) to steady them -
never breaking into a run, never losing their order, — and I
say, Then and there was the supreme exhibition of their
soldierly qualities!"[20]

Steuart's men regrouped at the base of the hill where
they were able to repel the Union pursuers. Artillery continued
to rain down upon them but for the moment, the tired and

exhausted soldiers were able to take a deep breath and with that, a renewal of spirit. "By the strenuous efforts of the officers of the line and of the staff, order was restored, and we re-formed in the breastworks from which we had emerged, there to be again exposed to an artillery fire exceeding in violence that of the early morning,"[21] reflected McKim. He then added, "if the tattered battle flag of the Third North Carolina was followed by only a handful, it was because they had already suffered more heavily than any other regiment."

As the Confederates retreated down the hill, they left behind their dead and wounded. At the base of the hill, Johnson's men rallied and quickly formed a line to repel the Union pursuit. "The men were rallied behind some large boulders of rock (the position they had just charged from), and were forced to retire, from the losses incurred in their charge against, and not before any charge of the enemy, to Rock creek, several hundred yards to the rear, where, posted as a heavy skirmish line, they continued the contest till night,"[22] reported Lieutenant Zollinger. There they put up a stiff resistance and finally at 10:15 AM, the Union blue pulled back and the battle for possession of Culp's Hill was over. One soldier remembered that General Steuart was heartbroken. Tears were rolling down his cheeks, he was heard repeatedly to exclaim: "My poor boys! My poor boys!"[23]

Whittier commented later: "No place on the field of Gettysburg presented such a terrible effect of battle as the portion of Culp's Hill in front of Greene's line and along the works vacated by McDougall's Brigade of the First Division. From close up under our works down the hill to the Creek. The open places between the boulders were covered with Confederate dead, every exposed place holding groups, and behind the rocks many wounded had been dragged only to die a lingering death."[24] In the meantime, Randolph McKim also reported much of the same: "What a field was this! For three hours of the previous evening, and seven of the morning, had the most terrible elements of destruction known to modern warfare been wielded with a might and dexterity rarely if ever paralleled. The woods in which the battle had been fought was torn and rent with shells and solid shot and pierced with innumerable Minie balls. Trees were broken off and splintered, and that entire forest, where the battle raged most furiously, was, on the following year, leafless, the stately but mute occupants having yielded up their lives with those whom they overshadowed."[25]

Many had yielded up their lives in the course of their beliefs and in response to the orders given. No man wants to die, but in the course of battle many do. After the fighting stops, and the wounded are attended, then the survivors must lay to rest those that had fallen in their noble endeavor. John Futch, who had remained by the side of his older brother, was now in the predicament of having to bury his older brother. Charley had remained conscious until near the end, and was in a tremendous amount of pain. Partly paralyzed, he could only communicate with his eyes, while John tried his best to comfort his older brother. The battle for Culp's Hill was over and several hours later, Charley's fight for life was also over. Charley died around 2 o'clock on the afternoon on July 3, as cannons elsewhere on the field exchanged volleys across a field that one day would immortalize and symbolize the Battle of Gettysburg.

John Futch was insoluble. All of his life, he had counted on his brother for advice, comfort and support and now he was gone. "I am at very great loss since the death of Charley. I am so lonesome I do not know what to do,"[26] he wrote to his wife. In another letter, he explained: "I haven [haven't] seen no plesher [pleasure] since Charley got kild [sic] I am at a grate [great] lost since I lost Charley til I am all most crasey [crazy] but I will get a long with it that I can."[27]

Later that night, burial parties were formed to bury the dead. John wanted to give Charley the proper respects as he reflected on his brother "Charley never spoke after he got woundid and he wanted to go home mity bad before he died . . . pore feler he got kild a long wase [ways] from home. I was very sory [sorry] that I codent [couldn't] get a cofen [coffin] to bearey [bury] him but I beared [buried] him the best I cod [could] it was something that I never expected to haft to do but we don't know what we will do tel [until] he gets in the world."[28] In the very next letter home, John once again wrote home and it was as if he was trying not only to console his family, but also himself: "we buried him on the night of the 3d. Only God knows the bitter anguish this sad berevement [bereavement] sent thrilling through my sad heart. It seems hard to part forever from those our heart treasures - but the Lords will be done - Let us put our trust in Him. He alone can comfort the grief stricken soul, and bind up the broken heart."[29]

---

[1] OR, Series 1 Vol. XXVII, pp.826-8.

[2] McKim, p.187.

[3] OR, Series II, Vol. XXVII, p. 510.

[4] Samuel P. Bates, *Battle of Gettysburg,* (Philadelphia, n.p., 1875), p.139.

[5] McKim, p.213.

[6] ibid., p.203.

[7] Zollinger, p. 106.

[8] McKim, p. 213.

[9] Zollinger, p. 106.

[10] McKim, p.200.

[11] ibid., p.188.

[12] Greene, p. 317.

[13] McKim, p. 189.

[14] ibid., p.204.

[15] Champ Clark, p.127.

[16] McKim, p.201; Bates, p. 142.

[17] McKim, p.186.

[18] ibid., p.205.

[19] ibid.

[20] ibid., p.186.

[21] ibid., p.205.

[22] Zollinger, p. 106.

[23] Thomas L. Elmore, "Courage Against the Trenches: The Attack and Repulse of Steuart's Brigade at Culp's Hill," *Gettysburg Magazine,* No. 7 (July, 1992) p. 95.

[24] Whittier, p. 348.

[25] McKim, p. 208.

[26] John Futch in letter to his wife, July 31, 1863.

[27] ibid., August 2, 1863.

[28] ibid.

[29] ibid., August 6, 1863.

Chapter Five

In Camp

After a murderous but magnificent fatal charge made on the afternoon of July 3, 1863, Lee was forced to withdraw from the Pennsylvania countryside. The carnage for both combatants of the three-day battle was in excess of fifty thousand men killed, wounded or missing. While burial details laid the dead to rest, carcasses of thousands of animals lay bloated on the field. Farmlands were turned into cemeteries as homes in the area served as hospitals. Many severely wounded Confederate soldiers were left behind as Lee hastened his army southward. The citizens of Gettysburg would care for the wounded and then it would be off to a prisoner of war camp for the survivors. By the late afternoon and evening of the fourth of July, a tremendous rainstorm swept the fields of Gettysburg. It was as if the Gods of War wanted to cleanse the land of the blood and, at the same time, conceal the tears of many on both sides of the conflict.

The road back to Virginia would be a long and hard one for the men of the Lee's army, especially for those who left behind family and friends on the fields of Gettysburg. Sadness and despair were felt everywhere, but the steadiness of the march, combined with officers maintaining strict decorum, gave a sense of security. Food was scarce as many of the wagons had either been destroyed or left behind. Some of the men had not eaten for days and many were unable to eat. Randolph McKim remembered: "During the whole march it rained hard, and the men had not one day's rations in the three."[1] At night, when allowed, fires were made to ward off the chill and to hasten the drying of wet and damp uniform items. "Fence rails were burned for the first time in Pennsylvania, and by permission," recalled McKim.

The nights were long and lonely, as sleep was illusive for many despite the fact they were on the verge of exhaustion. Many had to abandoned supplies and personal items on the battlefields and now had to do without. Those that did have shared with those that had not. As the 3d North Carolina pulled back, John Futch, like many, was at a complete loss. He had lost the most important thing in his life - his older brother. He also was suffering from chills and fever as were many of his messmates for the rain had soaked them through and through. The dampness and their fatigue contributed to their overall health. John Futch wrote his wife: "I am not well at this time [.] I have a bad cold and I am waried [sic] out a marching."[2]

Lee's army slowly moved toward Orange Court House. Scouts kept an eye on the pursuing Union army, which had been re-supplied and was well rested. As the weary Confederate soldiers began to trickle into the vicinity, the citizens of Orange County, once again, opened their hearts and their homes to the men. As thousands of tents sprung up on farms, and flags were unfurled, visitations and invitations were once more extended. For the men though, the marching was over and a sigh of relief felt. Men collapsed and fell to the ground in complete and utter exhaustion. It had been three long months since the start of the Chancellsorville and Gettysburg campaigns and, now for the time being, rest was at hand.

General Richard S. Ewell, commander of Lee's Second Corps, took his corps several miles south of Orange Court House and there made camp. Two of his three divisions were placed on or near the grounds of Montpelier, the home of James Madison, the fourth President of the United States. The division of Robert Rodes assumed a position along the banks of the Rapidan near Liberty Miles while Edward Johnson's Division was placed east of the Plank Road. Two of Johnson's brigades, George Steuart and James A. Walker, were actually encamped on the grounds of the former President's home.

Watkins Kearns, of the 27th Virginia, recalled on August 1, 1863 "many men give out owing to the heat. Marched to within 2 ½ miles of Orange Court House to the property of James Madison and camped."[3] At the same time, John O. Casler, of Johnson's Division, mentioned, "Our division was camped at Montpelier, President Madison's old homestead, a few miles from Orange Court House. As the weather was hot and dry, we did not have any work to do, but lay idle in camp and took a good rest, and recruited up after our severe campaigns."[4]

With the recent severe campaigns behind them, this was the time that both the men and the army desperately needed to rebuild both physically and mentally. It had been a long and very difficult campaign. The losses had been tremendous. Some of the men needed this time to sort things out in their minds. They had to reflect on what they had just gone through and what they had experienced. Hopefully, they would be able to find an inner strength needed to face what was to come. All knew the war was not over and there would be more fighting to come. They had to be ready for it.

Some of the soldiers had come from this area and had sought permission to visit family and friends. When they paid a visit to their homes and families, they often took with them close messmates and comrades. The need for closeness of family and home, especially for those whose homes were far away, was paramount. The local citizenry opened up their hearts to the men. Many residents extended invitations to Lee's top echelon and offered to share their homes with them. In the meantime, the officers remaining in camp tried to re-establish confidence and strength among the soldiers and at the same time, maintaining military affairs and discipline.

The army had lost a great many of its experienced commanders. Some companies had almost been annihilated in the last battle and they needed to be either rebuilt or combined with other companies, other regiments. Guns and ammunition had been either destroyed or left behind on the field and the army desperately needed to have them replaced or repaired. In addition, many horses and mules were also needed to replace those either killed or left behind. Portions of companies or regiments were sent home for recruitment duty while supplies filtered in for the next campaign.

Field and battle reports were written and reviewed. Orders were generated and military discipline observed. Drills and field exercises were held as were military reviews and courts-martial. Picket and skirmish duties were rotated among the brigades, and those assigned to such duties would be gone for days until relieved by the oncoming watch. Camp life began to quickly return to normal as did camp boredom. Steuart's Brigade was well known for its cleanliness for General Steuart demanded that his camps be maintained in a clean and orderly fashion. After all the appearance of a camp was indicative of the men; if the camp was clean, the men were sharp and on top of things; if the camp was dirty and shoddy, then the men would be that way in everything they do, especially in following orders during a battle. So in Steuart's camps, it was not unusual to see men, with switch brooms, sweeping the dirt of rocks and leaves. Upon completion of the task, the dirt resembled brown marble.

Those not on any assigned duty were free to go about their business, fish, reading books, writing letters. Some, receiving a pass, traveled to either Orange Court House or Gordonsville, or paid a visit to neighboring camps. Of course, the young soldiers were glad to receive invitations from the ladies. Numerous picnics and dances were held, and since some of the camps were in the vicinity of Montpelier, many soldiers visited the famous home of President James and Dolley Madison. The home was now under the ownership of Francis (Frank) Carson, who apparently made the home and grounds open to the visiting troops.

But, not all was gaiety. Camp life was hard. Orders were given and obeyed or discipline administered. John Futch, in a letter home, stated " I can only assure you we are living the worst life ever lived. Our rations are short and our duty hard."[5] In another letter, he revealed, "I have had one mes [s] of beans and squashes but I had to pay 1 dollar for them [.] I haven't had no money in more a month."[6] He concluded this letter by telling his wife, "I am comin [g] home the first chance I can get [.] I think that this war will end before long for I think that the yankes will whip us before long."

That was the feeling expressed by many of the men who were not only tired of war but also what they felt was the senseless loss of life. Many wanted the fighting to end so they could just go home. Many had lost their closest friends and some of the men had seen family members die in battle. Many had been wounded and some had experienced numerous wounds. There was no time to grieve for family or friends, much less themselves. They had seen not only their ranks

61

thinned by war, but had also observed much inefficiency and injustice.

Many men had received news of home telling of troubling times, shortfalls of crops and other problems. Wives and mothers urged their husbands and sons to come home. Some of the soldiers had not seen their homes or their families since they enlisted or were conscripted. Furloughs were hard to come by and, even if they got one, many men could not afford to go home. The salary for a private was eleven dollars a month and the cost of supplies high, leaving very little money for the expensive travel home.

After the loss of his brother, John Futch complained constantly of his loneliness in many of the letters that he had sent home to his wife and mother. His letters were full of despair and anguish and always telling them that he wanted so much to come home. He had apparently applied for furloughs only to be denied them. In desperation, after again being denied a furlough, he wrote his wife that he was coming home. "I would like to come home but I do not known when I will get the chance to come again. But I am going to come before long if I have to runaway to do it."[7]

John had also sought information of home and local news. Instead he received neither. When a letter did arrive, all he heard was of hardships, and loneliness. Martha, his wife, was trying to manage without him and raise his son from a previous marriage. In a letter dated August 16, he wrote to her saying, "Marthy I want to no [know] if you have drawn any money or not and if you havent [haven't] I want you to try to draw if you can [.] I have rote [wrote] to you all but I cant [can't] get any answers yet [.] Marthy I want to come home the worse I ever did in my life [.] I am very uneasy about you

- you must do the best you can for your self [.] I have got some money for you if I could send it to you but I am afraid to send it in a letter it is said our letters is broke open and red [read]."[8]

John's uneasiness about his wife was not uncommon. By now, the men had been away from home for a time and newspapers carried stories telling of the various battles and mentioning the number of casualties. Letters from home expressed families' concerns and worries for the men's safety. Many letters told how the family longed for the war to be over as husbands and fathers were desperately needed and missed. Some wives even made demands on their men, telling them that without their presence all was lost. The letters, full of sadness, despair and hopelessness, begged the men to come home now.

For the most part, the majority of the soldiers stayed and honored their obligations and commitments. There were a few though who had become disillusioned and disenchanted with army life and were looking for a way out of it. There were stories of soldiers who went so far as to maim or injure themselves, but this was rare. Many instead just simply walked away from their camp, their comrades, and the army and headed home.

There really isn't a justification for desertion. Desertion has plagued the military since the beginning of time. There were as many causes as there were soldiers. Very few of the reasons had to do with cowardice or fear of battle, but most were because of loneliness for home and family. At this particular time, desertion in the Confederate Army was increasing at an alarming rate and steps would have to be taken to stem the tide.

By late 1863, the soldiers of North Carolina had received, unjustly, a reputation for desertion. There were many factors that played in the background and all or some had an impact on the poor soldier who sat in camp and talked with their comrades of family, home and military life. Some had received news of home telling them of children's illness or even of their deaths. Others heard of crop failures at homes, or concerns were expressed from their wives about how were they to feed themselves or even cases where wives and children were being assaulted by neighbors or roving bands of thieves or thugs.

Editors and newsmen of certain North Carolinian newspapers wrote series of articles condemning the conscription laws. The conscription laws were established in 1862 to increase the enlistment of eligible men into military service for the defense of the young and struggling Confederacy. Certain opponents had argued that conscription was illegal and unconstitutional and, those conscripted were in reality civilians and not subject to military law or discipline for any infractions. Some papers went so far as to encourage desertion letting it be known that, especially in the western part of the state, they would be received by a compassionate, understanding citizenry. For those who were arrested for desertion, they would be tried in civilian courts by lenient judges who often would find the poor soldier not guilty of the offense.

In May 1863, General James Johnston Pettigrew addressed the issue in a letter to Governor Z. B. Vance, of North Carolina. "A certain class of soldiers is influenced by this condition of public opinion. They are told, as you can see by the letters, that they can desert with impunity; that the militia officers will not do their duty." Pettigrew concluded his letter by saying: "I write this to you because you are the only person in the State having sufficient influence, as I think, to reform matters. It is absolutely necessary to bring the public opinion again to the condition of patiently and manfully meeting those trials which every people struggling for independence must meet; and so far as the army is concerned, the best way to accomplish this is to convince them that a man who deserts them in the face of the enemy will be met at home with scorn and speedily returned to deserved punishment."[9]

By now, the Conscription Bureau had been in place for well over a year, and in charge of the North Carolina Bureau was Peter Mallett. Charles Peter Mallett, known as Peter Mallett, was born May 24, 1825, and had been in New York City when the war broke out in 1861. Returning immediately home to Fayetteville, he raised a company of men and offered their service to the young Confederacy. Upon its formation, the company was designated Company C and was assigned to the 3d North Carolina Infantry Regiment. Mallett, was named as its captain, and his young nephew, Charles Peter Mallett, "not yet seventeen years old," volunteered and was "commissioned its Junior Second Lieutenant"[10] in the same company and regiment. Soon after the Conscription Bureau was established, Peter Mallet resigned his commission with the 3d North Carolina and was appointed Major, Assistant Adjutant General on May 23, 1862 and named as Commandant of Conscripts for the State of North Carolina.

With the number of desertions increasing, it was apparent that sterner and tougher measures would have to be taken to reduce the rate. In early July 1863, the Conscript Office in Richmond, in an effort to meet this growing menace, issued a circular. In it was stated "The War Department looks to the agencies of conscription to arrest the growing evil," and it ordered the commandant of conscripts to enroll sufficient number of conscripts to patrol areas known to be used by deserters. As an inducement, it authorized paying the patrols the wages of a cavalryman and authorizing the issuance of arms if necessary. It was hoped that "the exercise of the necessary vigilance and activity many men many be returned to service and the evil of desertion effectually stopped."[11]

On July 30, 1863, Colonel William Lowrance, commander of Scales' Brigade of Pender's Division of the 3rd Corps, reported the desertion of fifty men from the 22nd and 38th North Carolina Regiments. This report was made to J.A. Engelhard, Lee's Assistant Adjutant General. Less than a month previous, these fifty men had been actively engaged at Gettysburg and, as part of Pender's Division, had charged into the fray on the afternoon of July 1. Two days later, they had participated in the ill-fated Pickett's charge where approximately 12,000 men had walked across an open valley into the mouths of spitting cannon sending forth death and destruction. Lowrance blamed the desertions on news reports from North Carolina saying, "It is that disgraceful 'pease' sentiment spoken of by the Standard. Some-thing should be done; every effort should be made to overhaul them, and everyone should be shot. Let us hope to check it now, for if this should pass by unnoticed, many more will soon follow."[12]

Upon receipt of Lowrance's report, Lee wrote to Secretary of War James A. Seddon mentioning "The officers attribute these desertions to the influence of the newspaper articles. I hope that something may be done to counteract these bad influences." Lee then requested additional help in patrolling the crossings to North Carolina by vigilant patrols. "From what I can learn, it would be well, if possible, to picket the ferries and brigades on James River and over the Staunton and Dan Rivers . . ... Many of these deserters are said to pass that way, and it would be a great benefit to the army to catch them, in order to make some examples as speedily as possible."[13]

On August 1, President Jefferson Davis issued a Proclamation hoping not only to inspire confidence in his troops, but also to enlist the help of local citizens to in encouraging those who had left the army to return. As an added incentive, he offered a general pardon to those deserters who returned to their respective commands. In his proclamation, Davis said:

> Those who are called to the field
> by every motive that can move the human
> heart should promptly repair to the post of
> duty, should stand by their comrades now
> in front of the foe, and thus so strengthen the
> armies of the Confederacy as to insure success.
> The men now absent from their post would, if
> present in the field, suffice to create numerical
> equality between our force and that of the
> invaders; and when with any approach to such
> equality have we failed to be victorious?   . . .
> I call on you, then, my countrymen, to hasten to
> your camps in obedience to the dictates of
> honor and of duty, and I do hereby declare that
> I grant a general pardon and amnesty to all
> officers and men within the Confederacy now
> absent without leave who shall with the least
> possible delay return to their proper posts of
> duty. [14]

Davis, in this same proclamation, sent a message to the wives and girlfriends enlisting their efforts to get the errant soldier back in the field and to his command. "Finally, I conjure my countrywoman, the wives, mothers, sisters, and daughters of the Confederacy, to use their all-powerful influence in aid of this call, to add one crowning sacrifice to those which their patriotism has so freely and constantly offered on their country's alter and to take care that none who owe service in the field shall be sheltered at home from the disgrace of having deserted their duty to their families, to their country and to their God."[15]

During the first few weeks of August, the men of Steuart's Brigade settled into a routine at their camp on the grounds of Montpelier near Orange Court House. Drill was held not only in the early morning hours prior to breakfast, but was followed by more drill in the afternoon and, every once in a while, an evening drill. There would be other various assignments, which quickly filled up the majority of the day for the soldier, and for the most part, evenings were spent amongst themselves.

Groups of men would gather together to talk and discussions on home and family took priority, as did the injustices of military life. While most had been good soldiers, a few had received punishments for minor infractions. Some had earned extra guard duty while others had carried a brick around for companionship as a reminder against further instances of goldbricking. Some had mounted the "wooden horse" as others had suffered from being tied up by the thumbs. Discussions also centered on military matters and the thought of future battles discussed. Many believed the war would end shortly while others saw the fruitlessness of it. Men talk about the possibility of leaving camp and the war and all of its hell behind and making tracks for home and family.

John Futch was not the only man in the 3d North Carolina Regiment who longed to be at home with his wife and family. So did William Barefoot, of Company H. Barefoot had not seen his wife, Elizabeth, or his three children since he enlisted on February 15, 1862. He missed them and, since leaving his home in Whiteville, North Carolina, had seen just about enough of the war that he cared too. Seven months after he enlisted, Barefoot was captured at Boonsborough, Maryland on September 15, 1862, just after the Battle of South Mountain. He was paroled four months later and, upon returning to his company, he once more took up the rifle. He was fed up with military life and wanted more than anything else to go home. He mentioned to a few close friends that he was thinking leaving and, as he did, he found there were others who felt the same way. Some asked if they might join him.

Barefoot's messmates listened to him. They also missed their families and they also longed for the comforts of home. Many had applied for furloughs, only to be denied them. Some had received letters telling of difficulties while others longed for word from a love one. It is unknown if anyone mentioned the possible consequences should they get caught. But the thought of home was strong and the more they thought of home, the more they wanted to go. A few who were thinking of leaving did not think they were actually deserting. For some of these soldiers had been conscripted and had not enlisted. Weren't the newspapers from home full of stories telling them that conscription was illegal and unconstitutional? As such, they could walk away. The plan was thus made and would soon be put into operation.

[1] McKim, p.182.

[2] John Futch, letter to his wife, July 19, 1863.

[3] Watkins Kearns, *Diary for May 17, 1863 – February 29, 1864,* [MSS5:1 K2143:3] (notation made August 1, 1863, [Copied at the Virginia Historical Society, Richmond, Virginia.

[4] John O. Casler, *Four Years in the Stonewall Brigade,* (Dayton, Oh, Morningside Bookshop, 1971), p 188.

[5] John Futch, July 15, 1963.

[6] ibid., August 2, 1863.

[7] ibid., July 31, 1863.

[8] ibid., August 16, 1863.

[9] OR, Series 1, Vol. LI/2, p. 714.

[10] Charles Beatty Overman, "My Grandfather: A Sketch" Mallett Genealogy Page [http://www.Ancestry.Com)].

[11] OR, Series IV, Vol. II, p. 618.

[12] ibid., Series I, Vol. XXVII/3, p. 1053.

[13] ibid.

[14] ibid., Series IV, Vol. II, p. 688.

[15] ibid.

Chapter Six

Going Home

Sometime around August 20th, approximately twelve men to fifteen men from Companies H and K of the 3d North Carolina Infantry Regiment, including John and Hanson Futch, left camp and "started for home in North Carolina, intending to resist arrest if molested."[1] They made their way out of camp, and headed southward leaving the war behind. When some of the men left camp, they took their weapons with them. This was in violation of General Order 104, which had been issued in 1862 to relieve the stress and frustration felt by the civilian populace in the vicinity wherever the army encamped. At the time the citizens had expressed concerns about the idea of soldiers walking about the towns and villages with loaded weapons. Farmers also expressed concerns when their livestock showed up missing. Paragraph II of General Order 104 stipulated: "Arms must not be carried from the camp, nor will mounted men in camps be permitted to ride their horses, except upon duty."[2]

In addition to Barefoot and Futch, Francis Benson was another who walked out of camp with the others. Benson was a twenty-six year old barrel-maker from Bladen County, assigned to Company H. Married to a young widow, Jane Sprague, he had been urged constantly to come home by his wife. She had born him a daughter in late 1862, but the baby died less than six months later. Jane had been married once before and had lost that husband along with two children from that marriage. With the loss of her third child, she desperately needed her man at home with her.

71

In Company H, there were three other Bensons besides Francis. It is unknown at this time whether or not if they were related, but all came from Bladen County. Archibald T. Benson, age 22, was killed at Gettysburg as the 3rd North Carolina stormed Culp's Hill on July 2. Another Benson was Thomas W.L. Benson, who had been hospitalized with typhoid fever in early 1863. On June 17, he was transferred to the hospital near Danville "where he deserted on August 15, 1863."[3] The third Benson was William W. Benson. He had been listed on the muster rolls as having deserted on June 4, 1863 when the company was camped near Hamilton Crossing, Virginia.

Using the back roads and traveling at night, the men made their way south toward the James River. It is unknown when their absence was first notice, but as soon as it was, Major William Murdock Parsley, the twenty-two year old regimental commander was immediately notified. The exact date the men left camp has not been determined. Company H listed the men as missing on August 20, while the records of Company K shows the date to be anywhere from August 11 to August 31. This time frame was when the company muster rolls were prepared in preparation for the paymaster. In all probability, the men left camp on or around August 20, for it was on August 20 that John Futch posted his last letter home to his wife, telling her: "I expect to be home before long."[4] Because of the natural of the absences and the seriousness of the number missing, Parsley passed along the information up his chain of command, and eventually the news found its way to the ears of Robert E. Lee.

Prior to the Gettysburg campaign, General Lee expressed concerned about straggling in his army, but his mind at the time was primarily focused on the upcoming campaign. Straggling had become a common occurrence in the army as many men simply wandered from camp or while on the march to secure either food, to plunder or to rest. Though it was common, it was frowned upon and in some companies discipline administered to the transgressors. As Lee and his army made their return from Gettysburg, many soldiers were tired, exhausted or injured or sick and were unable to keep up as the army made its way back to Virginia. For days after the army's arrival in Orange County, soldiers continued to filter in to rejoin their companies and their comrades.

Since returning from the killing fields of Pennsylvania, Lee had many issues to deal with concerning his army. One issue was that of straggling. He had seen a rise in the number of stragglers and desertion among his men since the spring campaigns. The number of desertions were on the rise as soldiers deliberately walked out of camp while others simply had not returned from their furloughs. It was an increasing problem and one that had to be dealt with. Lee aimed to tackle the problem. At first, he appealed to the men's sense of pride and responsibility when he issued General Order Number 80 on July 26, 1863. Newspapers throughout the Confederacy carried the article among the advertisements during the month of August.

Headquarters Army Northern Va.
July 26, 1863

General Order No. 80[5]

All officers and soldiers now absent from this army who are able to do duty and not detached on special service, are ordered to return immediately. The Commanding General calls upon all soldiers to rejoin their respective regiments at once. To remain at home in this hour of our country's need is unworthy the manhood of a Southern soldier. While you proudly boast that you belong to the Army of Northern Virginia, let it be not said that you deserted your comrades in a contest in which everything you hold dear is at stake. The Commanding General appeals to the people of the States to send forth every man able to bear arms to aid the brave soldiers who have so often beaten back our foe, to strike a decisive blow for the safety and sanctity of our homes, and the independence of our county.

By command of General R. E. Lee
R.H. Chilton A.A.A.I.G.

The day after its issuance, Lee wrote to President Jefferson Davis explaining his reason for the General Order. Expressing his concern. Lee informed Davis, "There are many thousand men improperly absent from this army. I have caused to-day an appeal to be made to them to return at once to duty. I do not know whether it will have much effect, unless accompanied by the declaration of an amnesty. I doubted the policy of this, but I would respectfully submit that perhaps a general amnesty declared by your Excellency might bring many delinquents back to the different armies of the Confederacy."[6]

Though President Davis had offered a pardon in his proclamation of August 1, he now issued General Order 109 in support of General Lee by granting the amnesty requested. The order was published in the newspapers throughout the South on August 11 and was carried on the front page. It proclaimed that all soldiers absent without leave or those who had not reported for service would be granted a pardon and amnesty if they reported within twenty days.

GENERAL ORDER NO. 109 [7]
Adjt. And Insp. General's Office
Richmond, August 11, 1863

I.   A general pardon is given to all officers and men within the Confederacy, now absent without leave from the army, who shall within twenty days form the publication of the address of the President in the State in which the absentees may then be, return to their posts of duty.

II.   All men who had been accused or convicted, and undergoing sentence for absence without leave or desertion, excepting only those who have been twice convicted of desertion, will be returned to their respective commands for duty.

By Order:
S. Cooper,
Adjutant and Inspector General

One deserter who had left camp prior to the Gettysburg campaign took advantage of this pardon and amnesty. He was Private Joseph R. Kemp, Company H of the 3d North Carolina. He had left camp along with William W. Benson on June 4, 1863 while the company was near Hamilton Crossing, Virginia. After hearing and reading of the pardon, he rejoined his company near Orange Court House, Virginia on August 14, 1863, with impunity. Several months later, Kemp was promoted to corporal and continued to do his duty. But the twelve to fifteen men who walked out of camp on August 20 did not return.

On August 15, General Lee wrote a letter to General Samuel Cooper, the Adjutant and Inspector General in Richmond. Cooper was the Superintendent of the Bureau of Conscription urging him to cooperate in "enrolling officers in causing to return to duty the number of soldiers wandering at large through the country, who should be with their commands in the field."[8] Two days later on August 17, Lee explained to President Davis the problem he was having with desertion in the army. "In one corps, the desertions of North Carolinians, and, to some extent, of Virginians, has grown to be a very serious matter. . . . General Imboden writes that there are great numbers of deserters in the valley, who conceal themselves successfully from the small squads sent to arrest them. Many cross the James River near Balcony Falls en route for the south, along the mountain ridges. Night before last, 30 went from one regiment and 18 from another. Great dissatisfaction is reported among the good men of the army at the apparent impunity of deserters."[9] He concluded this letter by suggesting "nothing will remedy this great evil which so much endangers our cause excepting the rigid enforcement of the death penalty in future in cases of conviction."

At the same time, Lee wrote to General John D. Imboden, commander of the Valley District. "There is much desertion, I regret to say, from this army, principally from the North Carolina troops, but it also occurs among others." He ordered Imboden to "try to ascertain their lurking places, send parties for their capture, and disperse them," and concluded with the same recommendation he had made to Davis: "I begin to fear nothing but the death penalty, uniformly, inexorable administered, will stop it."[10]

Squads of armed troops were dispatched to areas where suspected deserters were known to pass. One group of soldiers, under the command of Adjutant Lieutenant Richardson Mallett, had been detached from the 46th North Carolina and sent to Scottsville, Virginia. This area, on the James River, was well known for its ferries and river crossings and was surrounded by dense woods, which provided cover for men trying to conceal themselves from armed patrols. Mallett and his small squadron of men would patrol the area searching for deserters and if they found any suspicious or errant soldier trying to cross the James River, they would detained and arrested them.

Richardson Mallett, born on September 12, 1840, had been a student at the University of North Carolina at Chapel Hill prior to the war. He had enrolled in the fall of 1858, and according to his school transcripts, his course of study was heavy in mathematics, languages and the Bible. Listed as "tolerable to respectable,"[11] Mallett left school after his June examinations in 1861 to enlist in the Confederate army.

The Mallett family of Fayetteville was well represented in the Confederate army. Richardson, along with several older brothers and a young nephew, three years his junior, quickly signed up in the summer of 1861. Richardson joined the Orange Light Infantry, as a lieutenant in Company D, 1st North Carolina. His older brother, Charles Peter Mallett, known as Peter, was named captain of Company C of the 3d North Carolina, and later was became Commander of Conscripts for North Carolina. Another older brother, Edward Jones Mallett, enlisted in the 61st North Carolina while his nephew, the son of his brother Charles Beatty Mallett, had joined the 3d North Carolina with his Uncle Peter.

Richardson Mallett saw his military first action on June 10, 1861 during the Battle of Bethel. He "was then put in charge of transportation boats on the York River. He remained at Yorktown until these volunteers were discharged, after six months service."[12] Upon being discharged from the 1st North Carolina, he was quickly appointed as a Lieutenant of artillery and saw active service when Union forces under General Burnside drove back Confederate forces at New Berne, North Carolina in March 1862.

After New Berne, Mallett was named Adjutant in Holt's Battalion, of the 46th North Carolina. "In May his regiment was ordered to the battlefield of the Chickahominy; than all through the Maryland campaign, the capture of Harper's Ferry."[13] Mallett had earned the praise of his commander, Colonel E. D. Hall, for performance during the Battle of Sharpsburg [Antietam]. In his report filed on October 3, 1862, Hall stated "Adjutant [R] Mallett also performed his duties with great abilities."[14]

Mallett, along with the 46th North Carolina, was transferred in the spring of 1863 to the Army of Northern Virginia, "where they remained in the defenses around Richmond."[15] In August, Mallett was ordered to take a small contingent of men to the Scottsville area where they were to detain and/or arrest any stragglers or deserters that happened to cross their path. This was in response to the urgent pleas of both General Imboden and General Lee.

Mallett was informed that most of the illegal crossings of the fords took place either late at night or early in the morning hours. A little pass one in the morning of Tuesday, August 25, 1863, the young Adjutant led a detachment of soldiers toward a crossing near Bowling's Landing where it was reported that a group of men had been sighted. It was believed that these men might be deserters and Mallett had to verify and, if they were, place them under arrest. The detachment came upon the band as the group was making its way across the ford. Spotting them, Mallett ordered them to halt. As he did, shots rang out. Mallett had run across the men of the 3rd North Carolina Regiment who were bound and determined to make it across the ford. They were going to go home. They would resist if challenged and challenged they were. One or two of the men opened fire and, as they did, their first round struck the Lieutenant in the chest. As Mallett fell to the ground, his troops opened fire on the deserters, and for a few minutes, the area was alive with the sounds of gunfire, orders being barked as men scattered everywhere.

In the fire fight that followed, several of the deserters were killed, another was seriously wounded and several escaped into the woods. But there were ten men who threw down their weapons and were taken prisoner. It is believed that two of the deserters who were killed may have been William R. Stell, age 29, and James A. Tuter, age 19, both of Company K. No records could be located on these men, but their service records indicate that they deserted around August 11, 1863, and it is probable that they were the ones killed in the arrest attempt. The wounded man, Hanson Futch, of Company K, along with the severely wounded Lieutenant Mallett, was taken to the hospital in Scottsville. Mallett succumbed to his wounds six hours later. As he was dying, according to his family, he said "tell the colonel I was doing my duty, God's will be done. Amen."[16] The prisoners, including the wounded man, were transported to Richmond the next day and confined in Castle Thunder, under guard. They would be tried as soon as possible not only for desertion, but also for the murder of Adjutant Mallett.

Mallett's body was prepared for shipment home to Fayetteville, North Carolina where his family still resided. The Fayetteville Observer reported the young adjutant's death stating "He established a reputation for gentleman; and soldierly qualities of the highest order. . . . Of excellent capacity and disposition, devoted to his country and fearless in its cause, he was respected alike by officers and men. Few men of his years made or deserved so many loving friends, and none has died whose loss will be more sincerely lamented by his old comrades."[17] Mallett was buried on Saturday, August 29th in the family cemetery, which is today located behind the State Highway Commission on Gillespie Street in Fayetteville, North Carolina.

---

[1] Casler, p.189.

[2] OR, Series IV, Vol. II, p.235.

[3] *Carolina Troops: 1861-1865: A Roster,* compiled by Louis H. Mararian, Vol. III, p. 567.

[4] John Futch, August 20, 1863.

[5] OR, Series I, Vol. XXVII/3, p. 1040; Richmond Enquirer dated August 21 and August 25, 1863 [copied at the Virginia Historical Society and The Alderman Library, University of Virginia, Charlottesville, Virginia].

[6] OR, Series I, Vol. XXVII/3, p. 1041.

[7] ibid., Series I, Vol. XXIX/2. P. 642.

[8] ibid., p. 648.

[9] ibid., p. 650.

[10] ibid.

[11] Grades and Attendance Record, Richardson Mallett, 1858-1861. Transcribed by the University Student Records, Scholarship 1852-1866, v. 3 University Affairs, Student Records and Faculty Reports, Subgroup 1, Academic Records, University Archives and Records Service, Wilson Library, University of North Carolina at Chapel Hill, Chapel Hill, North Carolina.

[12] Stephen B. Weeks, ed., "Biographical Sketches of the Confederate Dead of the University of North Carolina, *North Carolina University Magazine,* New Series, V. IX, No. 2 pp 81-82.

[13] ibid.

[14] OR, Series I, Vol. XIX/1, p. 919.

[15] North Carolina Troops, Vol. VIII, p. 131.

[16] Cumberland County Survey, Fayetteville Genealogy Society, Vol. 1, p. 52; Fayetteville Observer SW dated August 31, 1863, [copied at the Stae Archives, Raleigh, North Carolina].

[17] ibid.

Chapter Seven

The Ultimate Penalty

Escorted under guard, the ten shackled prisoners arrived the next day in Richmond where they were immediately confined on the second floor of the notorious prison known as Castle Thunder. Before the war, Castle Thunder had been known as Greanor's Tobacco Factory, which was a large tobacco warehouse located on the north side of Cary Street in Richmond. Converted to a prison in1862, the factory was renamed Castle Thunder, the name being derived from mythology "indicative of Olympian vengeance upon offenders against her laws and one which, in point, is a good as any other that could be chosen, Castle Grizzly not excepted."[1]

Castle Thunder served as a prison for not only convicted thieves and murderers, but also served as a hospital for captive injured or wounded soldiers. The prison hospital, located on the upper floors of the factory, was created in late 1862 for "it was found very difficult to convey invalids back and forth from the Libby prisoner hospital, which has been heretofore used for the reception of the sick among the prisoners at the Castle."[2] But when the influx of Union prisoners being confined in Libby Prison created an overcrowding condition, Confederate deserters, traitors and spies were moved from Libby and transferred to Castle Thunder.

Inmates of Castle Thunder were murderers, thieves and other criminals and were often referred to as "wharf rats from New Orleans" and "pug - uglies from Baltimore," by Captain

George W. Alexander, the commandant or warden of the prison. But with the introduction of the scum of the military - traitors, spies and deserters, George W. Thomas, a detective on Alexander's staff said that now there was another classification of prisoner confined in Castle Thunder: "A third class is the offensive soldiers who are the great majority."[3]

The prison earned a repetition for one of terror depending upon on a person's circumstances. According to John Caphart, a prison guard, "It was really dangerous for the officers to go among the prisoners, some of them were such desperate characters. A new prisoner sent in among them was usually knocked down, beat and robbed if he had anything about him."[4] While on the other edge of the spectrum, prisoners confined in the walls of the Castle were treated, according to some, cruelly and inhuman, while others believed that the inmates were treated in accordance to their behavior.

It was not uncommon for visitors to the prison to see a man bucked and gagged in the hallways. According to T.G. Bland, a hospital steward at the prison, "the 'gag' is effected by a stick inserted crosswise in the mouth and the 'buck' is to tie the arms at the elbows to a cross-piece beneath the knees." [5] Accounts varied as to how long a man would be kept in this position with reports varying from sunup to sundown, while others reported that it was more like two to three days.

In addition to the buck and gag, other forms of discipline or punishment were administered at not only Castle Thunder but other prisons as well. One punishment often administered was known as the barrel shirt, which was used more for humiliation than anything else. "The shirt is made by sawing a common flour barrel in twain and cutting armholes in the sides and an aperture in the barrel for the insertion of the wearer's head."[6]

Serious infractions though were handled by either tying the prisoners up by the thumbs, or having the prisoner whipped or flogged. One of the prison guards, J.F. Schaffer, recalled that tying a prisoner up by the thumbs was called "trusting up" and was at one time considered a sailor's punishment. Whippings were often administered on the upper floors of the tobacco factory and were done with a heavy thick strap according to Robert B. Crow, a detective on the warden's staff. Prisoners, when whipped, were given anywhere from twelve to fifty lashes depending on the offense. Sometimes, though, prisoners were "turned out in the Castle yard and kept there for two or three days. This latter punishment removed the prisoners to an outside yard, without benefit of cover nor blanket in all type of weather, and some of them were thinly and badly clothed and others were well clad."[7]

In April 1863, Captain George Alexander, the commandant of Castle Thunder, was summoned before a committee of the House of Representatives of the Confederate States to answer questions concerning the treatment of prisoners under his control. Alexander had been accused of "harshness, inhumanity, tyranny, and dishonesty," in the treatment of the prisoners. Various officers and prisoners were summoned to testify during the hearing and, upon its conclusion, Alexander was exonerated of all misconduct citing "the hard-bitten character of the inmates as justification for his behavior."[8]

John Caphart remembered that at the prison on "the second story there is a large hall and beyond that large-sized rooms where citizens and disloyaled persons are confined, and

85

on the third floor is a very large room for the soldiers and partitioned cells or rather rooms for the prisoners tried by court-martial and prisoners awaiting trial by court-martial."[9] In all likelihood, this would have been the place where the ten men of the 3d North Carolina were held as they awaited their day in court. Since records could not be located for the trial, the exact date of the hearing is unknown but would have been held either on Wednesday, September 2nd or Thursday, September 3. It is also unknown exactly how many officers sat in judgement.

Normally, a court martial panel hearing capitol offenses was often made up of from three to thirteen officers and it would take a two-thirds vote of all officers present to convict the accused. At this time, I have been unable to locate any record of the indictments, the proceedings or, for that matter, the testimony offered. Records of various proceedings for the Second and Third Corps are hard to find, but records of courts martial held in the First Corps can be located in the Museum of the Confederacy in Richmond. In the case of the men from the 3d North Carolina, with the exception of the wounded man, the trial was held quickly and the verdict returned almost immediately. The men were present for the trial but had been taken back to their cells to await the jury's decision on charges of murder and desertion. There would be only one verdict — guilty on all charges.

The men were not advised of the verdict much less the sentence. All they knew for sure was that they were to be sent back to their regiment under guard. There they would await their future. In the meantime, the final decision of the court was forwarded to the president. In court martial proceedings, especially those involving a capitol offense such as this, the results had to be sent not only to President Jefferson Davis, but also to the Secretary of War, James A. Seddon. The court had decided that the men would pay the supreme penalty and it was to be death by musketry. [Hanging was the usual mode of execution for traitors and/or spies whereas the firing squad was reserved as the method for deserters.]

The Richmond newspapers reported the results of the trial on Friday, September 4. The Richmond Daily Dispatch announced that the men were to be "hung on the morrow." When the sentence was first announced, it had been decided that the men were to be executed at the prison in Richmond. However, because desertion had become so rampant, it was thought best to have the sentence carried out in front of the entire division. It was hoped that the sight of mass execution would stem the tide of desertion among the soldiers and would serve as an example of the fate that awaited those who deserted in the future. That same day, the Richmond Examiner, another Richmond paper, reported the execution "was to have taken place at Camp Lee immediately, but it being intimated that the execution should take place in the presence of the whole army of Northern Virginia, the condemned will be sent there and expatiate their crimes in the midst of their brothers in arms, whom they so basely deserted."

"About sundown, a party of 10 prisoners were brought, under guard from Richmond, to our headquarters,"[10] reported Lieutenant McHenry Howard, General Steuart's Acting Assistant Adjutant General. On duty as Duty Officer when the word was received, Howard sent a squad from the Provost Guard to meet the train carrying the prisoners when it arrived in Gordonsville on the evening of September 4. The prisoners were quickly and quietly escorted under guard to brigade headquarters, which is believed to have been a mile or two north of where the Montpelier mansion is located today. According Howard, Steuart's Brigade had been "situated between the road from Liberty Mill to Orange Court House (on the south) and the Rapidan River (on the north) and about three miles westerly from the Court House. Montpelier, President Madison's old home and a fine estate, was about a mile to the south and sometimes gave its name to the camp, but at our headquarters we called it 'Camp on Poplar Run,' from a small tributary of the Rapidan, on or near which, and near its mouth, our brigade was."[11]

Close to 9 P.M., a courier arrived from Richmond carrying orders from Major Robert W. Hunter, General Edward Johnson's twenty-six year old Assistant Adjutant General. Hunter, a former teacher, had enlisted in Company D of the 2nd Virginia at the outbreak of hostilities. He was later named as an adjutant and in 1862 served on General John B. Gordon's staff. In My, 1863, he was transferred to Johnson's staff. Howard received the courier and opened the sealed envelope immediately. Inside were the orders of the court. The court's decision was that all ten men were "to be shot to death by musketry at such time as the commanding general shall appoint,"[12] which was to be at 4 P.M., the following day, Saturday, September 5. Howard recalled "with this came a direction that the sentence should not be communicated to the prisoners until the morning of the day fixed for the execution."[13] He remembered that he was also to "take all possible means to secure them, handcuffing or tying them,"[14] and was instructed to "give your officer of the guard strict charges to allow no persons to communicate with the prisoners tonight."

Howard issued instructions for the order of the court to be carried out. The orders would be strictly followed. There would be no exceptions. The guard was doubled and orders issued to make sure that no one was to have any access to the prisoners. In addition to not having any visitors, the prisoners would not be allowed to communicate with anyone, including the guards. To prevent any possible escape or violation of the orders, the men were kept shackled and at all time remained in view of an armed guard.

The court-martial board had decided the execution was to take place in front of the entire division. General Johnson had enclosed a "Plot of Execution" long with the note from Hunter. This "Plot of Execution" contained a drawing showing where Johnson wanted each of his brigades to be posted during the execution. Howard was informed that Major Edwin L. Moore, Johnson's A.A.G. and Inspector General, would arrive early in the morning in order to assist with the preparations.

Howard welcomed any assistance he could get for it was hard to execute a man, but to shoot ten men at the same time in front of the entire division was indeed unusual and would be very difficult. Officers often had to order the death of men in the course of battle, for in wartime, men are lost and killed as they go forth on orders from their commanders. All officers are aware of this fact of life. Now, Howard was holding an order in his hands to cause the death of ten men – ten men who were members of his own brigade. He disliked the idea, "but such desertions - to the rear, not to the enemy - were increasing and it was necessary to make a stern example. And the crime of these men in going off armed, resisting and firing on the party sent to bring them back and killing the officer, was a heinous one."[15]

Early the next morning, Howard, along with the Reverend George Patterson and Major Moore, went to the guardhouse where the prisoners had been kept overnight. The prisoners were still shackled and it was apparent that some had not slept. Before their arrival, Howard had informed the others of the orders. They were also advised that the sentence would be carried out later that day. Patterson was asked to remain with the men and to offer them what comfort he could. Howard recalled: "I went to the guard quarters and had the ten men brought out and stand in line before me and read to them all the court martial record, with the final order that the sentence be carried into execution that day at 4 o'clock. I could not bear to look at them but I felt that no man stirred while I read. I was told that several of these men had been good soldiers and some had lately marched back from Gettysburg barefooted or nearly so."[16]

It was a trying time for all. The men were going to their deaths in a few hours. Some are believed to have suspected it, but others were shocked by the announcement. Punished yes, but few did not think they would have to forfeit their lives. Forfeit their lives? Unheard of! They had seen and heard of deserters before. There were many who had left the 3d North Carolina and had either returned on their own or been captured. None had received this type of punishment. It was understandable that the death penalty was to be administered for the killing of the adjutant, but not all had fired; not all had taken their weapons with them and not all were guilty of murder. As for the charge of desertion, no one was hurt. Why should they be put to death for that?

In the past, desertion was usually met by some form of punishment ranging all the way from complete forgiveness to being drummed out of the military. The men had seen it. The most severe punishment they had either seen or heard of had been inflicted on a deserter the year before. It was to one of their own, a fellow member of the 3d North Carolina. In late April 1862, Private James McKinlass, of Company D, had deserted, but was soon caught and brought back to face charges of desertion. Tried in Richmond before a court-martial on May 7, 1862, McKinlass was sentenced to receive thirty-nine lashes and "drummed out of the regiment, May 1862." Others in the meantime had deserted and were welcomed back with little or no penalty. A few had been branded with the letter "D" on their left hip, others had spent time in prison while still others were seen digging ditches, or marching a post for hours on end. However, no one had been shot for wanting to go home and getting away from this terrible war.

Patterson told the men that he would stay with them until the time of execution. Patterson, "a Greek by birth," was a Protestant-Episcopal Chaplain and had immigrated to the United States before the start of the war. When the war clouds loomed over the country and men were taking sides, Patterson elected to join with the young Confederacy. At the time of his enlistment, he resided in Washington County, North Carolina. In February 1863, the Reverend was assigned to the 3d North Carolina regiment and became a prominent member of Steuart's brigade. In 1864, he would transferred to Chimborazo Hospital in Richmond where he conducted the opening prayers of the Confederate Congress during the closing months of the war.

After hearing of the sentence, the men, with Reverend Patterson, moved inside the guardhouse to make their final preparations. Patterson heard them men's confessions and helped them write their final letters home. Additional guards were posted around the guardhouse as Major Moore met with

Lieutenant Howard and instructed him on how the execution would take place. In the meantime, a detail was drafted from General James A. Walker's brigade to prepare the place of execution.

In the orders received by Howard, Hunter had written: "For the firing parties, the Genl thinks you had better select men from other Regiments than the one to which the prisoners belong & select good men."[17] Thus, it was decided that all parties involved in the execution would come from other brigades in the division rather than from Steuart's Brigade. Though often a brigade was quite large consisting of several hundred men, the men were acquainted with one another. They marched and drilled together and often fought beside one another in various battles or skirmishes. Private John Casler, of the 33rd Virginia in Walker's Brigade, was part of the group given orders to prepare the execution site. He later recalled: "We planted ten posts in the ground, about three feet high and about fifty feet apart, all in line, boring a hole in each post near the top, and putting in a cross- piece."[18] Afterwards, according to Casler, "We dug one large grave in the edge of the woods, large enough to hold the ten coffins."[19]

By 3:30 P.M., Johnson's division had arrived at the site chosen for the execution. The four thousand men of the division quickly formed into a hollow square. The men were positioned along three sides of the square while the fourth side was left opened. It was in this open portion where the ten posts were located. In a military formation, a hollow square was used when infantry was faced with a cavalry charge. The actual formation would be a drawn up with the men making a square facing outward to meet the charge. Inside the square would be the regiment's colors, drums, baggage, etc.

General Edward Johnson, accompanied by his staff, arrived soon afterwards. As he sat stiffly in the saddle, his eyes took in the field before him. It was a troubling time. Nerves were on edge and the situation was one in which no one wanted to be involved in or with, but it was necessary. Johnson had a habit of winking one eye when he was in a state of agitation and on this day, everyone was in a state of agitation or close to it. The command staff immediately took their position in the center of the square near the colors. A few minutes later, "the prisoners were then brought from the guard-house, conducted by a heavy guard, accompanied by the Chaplain and surgeons," reported Private Casler. "As the column entered the field they were headed by the fifers and drummers — the drums being muffled — playing the dead march."[20] At the very end of the procession came members of the firing squad.

The firing squad consisted of one hundred twenty men. One hundred men composed the actual firing squad while the remaining twenty made up the reserve squad. It would be the responsibility of the reserve squad "to finish the execution should any of the condemned men not be killed at the first fire."[21] Before the execution, the officer of the guard had prepared the weapons to be used by the firing squad. Half of the guns were loaded with live ammunition; the other half was left empty. Afterwards, he prepared the rifles of the reserve squad, loading each with ball ammunition. The firing detail was divided into ten groups of ten men each – one squad for each of the condemned. Each member was issued a rifle, five with a fully loaded gun, the other five with an empty one. No one, except for the reserve squad, would know which he held until it came time to fire it. Only then, would members of the firing squad know if it was their shot or not that took the life of a comrade.

It was a very solemn occasion as the entourage came into view, with each group maintaining dignity and military bearing. One side of the square parted to let the group in and, everyone including officers, guards and the prisoners kept perfect step. The prisoners were paraded along the three sides of the square. As they walked, their eyes remained focused straight ahead. A reporter for the Richmond Daily Dispatch, who was present at the time, recalled in his story that was filed September 10: "The bearing of the prisoners was calm and self-possessed, and they marched to the place of their execution with a step as accurate in its cadence as that of the guard who conduced them." Many of those standing in the ranks kept their glaze downward and would not look at the men going to their deaths. Some had been friends with the condemned while others steadied their nerves to witness this spectacle of death.

As the men arrived at the open end of the square, the order was given to halt. It would fall to the Officer of the Day to read the charges and carrying out the actual execution. On this day, that position fell to Major Henry C. Wood of the 37th Virginia. He had assumed command of the 37th Virginia after its commander, Colonel T.V. Williams, fell wounded during the Battle of Chancellsorville. Now, Major Wood dismounted and stepped forward to "read the orders reciting their offenses, their sentences and the time and place of their execution."[22] Reverend Patterson, who had accompanied Wood, then proceeded to conduct a small service for the men. In the meantime, those standing in the ranks waited and watched. Many in the ranks were veterans of many campaigns, but this was something entirely different. It was an emotional time for all and at times, the silence on the field was deafening. Every once in a while, a word from the prayer services being held for the condemned. When the service was over, the Provost

Guards escorted each man to one of the posts anchored in the ground on the fourth side of the square. Each man was then placed on his knees with his back to the post. His arms were pinioned over the top rail and his hands tied in front of him. After the prisoner was secured to the post, a bandage was wrapped around his eyes and his hat placed over the bandage. All was now in readiness.

In the meantime, the ten firing squads assumed their position six paces directly in front of each post. A two-man reserve squad took their place to the rear of each detail. All was now quiet and then the pleas of the men tied to the posts could be heard. Some were crying for mercy while another was heard crying out "Oh, my poor mother." Others could be heard sobbing and some were heard deep in prayer. One cried out, "Oh, save me, save me."

Finally the appointed time arrived. It was 4 P.M. and Major Wood called the firing squad to attention. The drums rolled and then silence enveloped the field. The orders were given in a loud, crisp voice: "Ready! Aim!" and, after a slight pause, "Fire!" A single volley rang out as the guns discharged their deadly projectiles. The bullets found their mark, and ten bodies slump forward held in place by the ropes that affixed them to the posts to which they were fastened. Major Wood, along with the surgeons, walked forward and examined each man. They found two to five of the men still alive, having survived the first onslaught. A reporter for the Richmond Examiner described what happened next:

> It is discovered that all of the condemned
> have not been killed — some are only
> wounded; and then the most revolting part
> of the whole affair transpires. The reserves,
> of which there were two to each squad are

ordered up and they have to kill those whom
the volley has only wounded. Some six
or eight successive shots are fired in this way,
showing that probably some one at least had to
be fired at probably as often as three times.[23]

As soon as it was determined and confirmed that all
ten men were dead, the soldiers standing in the ranks were
ordered into columns of two. They were then marched pass the
sight of execution where the bodies of the deserters were still
suspended from the posts per instructions contained in the
orders from Richmond which stipulated: "The Brigades will
be marched by the flank by the corpses as they move from the
field to their quarters." [24] As the men moved by the posts, the
order, "Eyes right!" was given and the entire division took in
the terrible, tragic scene. The soldiers then were marched back
to their camps where they would reflect on what had unfolded
before their eyes. Many that evening had a difficult time
digesting their evening meal.

As the troops left the field, a detail from the 33rd
Virginia brought up the wagons carrying the coffins. "It was
our duty to untie them, place them in the coffins and load them
in the wagons,"[25] reported Private Casler. "The one that I
helped to put away had received four bullets in his breast, and
the rope that his hands were tied with was cut apart by a
bullet." The bodies were placed in individual coffins. As each
man was placed in his coffin, he was laid on his stomach with
his back facing upwards. Since the deceased turned his back
on his comrades and deserted, he would thus spend eternity
with his back to the world. Once the bodies were in placed, the
lids were secured and the coffins driven a short distance to the
site where the mass grave had been previously dug. The men
were then laid to rest in the woods near Poplar Run. As Casler

concluded "it cast a gloom over the entire army, for we had never seen so many executed at one time before."[26]

The next day the papers carried the news of the execution. The Richmond Daily Dispatch of September 7, 1863, reported the news but ended their article by saying the execution "terminated the existence of the wretched creatures who had shamefully abandoned the standards of their country and imbrued their hands in the blood of a gallant officer." The existence of the ten men who were executed on September 5, 1863 had indeed been terminated, for today it is difficult to find or locate any record or reference to them. The same applies to the wounded man, Hanson Futch. Having been severely wounded, he remained in the hospital at Castle Thunder while the other ten were returned to their regiment and execution. Hanson Futch also had been sentence to death, but his execution would have to wait until he was well enough to be tied to a post and shot. He remained in the hospital under the sentence of death until December 17, 1863 when he succumbed to smallpox, which he was exposed to while in the hospital.

---

[1] Castle Thunder, Richmond Enquirer of August 12, 1862, [copied from Internet Site: http://www.mdgorman.com/castle_thunder.htm, America on Line, August, 2001.
[2] Castle Thunder Hospital, Richmond Examiner of November 10, 1862 [copied from Internet Site: http://www.mdgorman.com/castle_thunder.htm, America on Line, November, 2001].
[3] OR, Series LL, Vol. V. p. 882; Castle Thunder Prison [copied from Internet Site: http://www.Wtv-zone.com/civilwar/castle.thun.html. America on Line, August 2001.
[4] OR, Series LL, Vol. V. p. 874.
[5] OR, Series LL, Vol. V, p. 883.
[6] ibid.
[7] ibid.

[8] Southern Historical Papers, *The Southern Historical Papers,* 52 Volumes, [CD-ROM] (Carmel, In, Guild Press of Indiana) Vol. XLIX, p. 90.

[9] OR, Series LL, Vol. V, p. 876.

[10] McHenry Howard, *Recollections of a Maryland Confederate Soldier and Staff Officer under Johnston, Jackson and Lee,* (Dayton, Oh., Mornigside Bookshop, 1975), p. 225.

[11] ibid., p. 224.

[12] ibid., p. 225.

[13] ibid.

[14] R.W. Hunter, letter to General G.H. Steuart dated September 4, 1863. (Copied at the Eleanor S. Brockenbrough Library, Museum of the Confederacy, Richmond, Virginia.)

[15] Howard, p. 226.

[16] ibid.

[17] R.W. Hunter, letter dated September 4, 1863.

[18] Casler, p. 189.

[19] ibid.

[20] ibid.

[21] ibid., 190.

[22] "The Military Execution on Saturday, *Richmond Dispatch,* September 10, 1863. (Copied at the Virginia Historical Society, Richmond, Virginia.)

[23] "From Lee's Army," *Richmond Enquirer,* September 15, 1863. (Copied at the Alderman Library, University of Virginia, Charlottesville, Virginia.)

[24] R.W. Hunter, letter dated September 4, 1863.

[25] Casler, p. 190.

[26] ibid.

Chapter Eight

The Aftermath

Who were the men who deserted their comrades in arms and paid the supreme price for their actions? In looking for what records are available in North Carolina, Virginia, and in Washington, most references pertaining to these men are no longer available. Some undoubtedly were destroyed in 1865 when Richmond burned. Others, particularly those in North Carolina, have also been destroyed. Most birth records before 1913 no longer exist. The question that needs to be asked is do these men deserve any mention or should they be forgotten and confined to the deep recesses of the earth?

One answer can be found in a speech made by Chaplain John Parks in 1864. He spoke out after witnessing the death of twenty-two deserters, also from North Carolina, who had not only left camp, but had also taken up the uniform and armaments of the foe. In that speech, Parks said:

And here allow me to say, I am not sufficiently
skilled in language to command words to express
the deep and unutterable detestation I have
of the character of a deserter. If my brother were
to be guilty of such a high crime, I should
certainly make an effort to have his name
changed to something else, that I, and my
children after me, might not feel the deep
and lasting disgrace which his conduct had
enstamped upon it. I hold, gentlemen, that
there are few crimes in the sight of either
God or man, that are more wicked and
detestable than desertion. The first step in

it is perjury. Who would ever believe such
an one in a court of justice again? The
second, is treason. He has abandoned the
flag of his country; thus much he has
aided the common enemy. These are
startling crimes, indeed, but the third
is equally so. He enstamps disgrace upon
the name of his family and children.[1]

Prior to leaving camp, the ten men of the 3d North
Carolina were good soldiers and had fought hard in numerous
campaigns against insurmountable odds as did the majority of
the soldiers on both sides. They were young men far from
home and lonely. Some had seen members of their own
families die in battle and some had learned of the deaths of
wives, parents, siblings and even their own children. In a
moment of vulnerability, they listened to others, believed in
what they had seen in the newspapers, and walked out of
camp, taking their weapons with them. Their crime was a
horrible one, especially in time of war. They deserted. They
wanted to go home and, in that effort, they killed a young,
valiant and gallant officer. In this case, they did take up arms
against their own. They paid the supreme penalty for their
actions and unfortunately they also sealed the fate of their
existence. "Disloyalty is a crime that mankind never forget
and but seldom forgive; the grave cannot cover it,"[2] related
Captain Parks.

Did witnessing the spectacle of the execution have any
effect on their fellow soldiers, especially those who knew
them, who served with them in the same company, the same
regiment? The men of the 3d North Carolina had witnessed
the death of their comrades and had seen their bodies dangling
from a post, held in place by a rope. It was meant as a warning

of future transgressions. The sight of ten men going to their death at the same time was, it is believed, would have a far reaching effect on others who might have entertained such thoughts as running away from responsibility and the honor of "doing your duty." It was thought that desertions would stop after such a traumatic and emotional occurrence. But it did not.

The execution took place on September 5, 1863. Less than a month later, the 3d North Carolina was on the move once more, this time eastward, as the Army of Northern Virginia became engaged in other skirmishes and other battles. The two months following the Battle of Gettysburg, both George G. Meade and Robert E. Lee attempted to rebuild their forces, their moral and their spirits. Meade's army was encamped near Culpeper while Lee's army remained close to Orange Court House. In late September, General James Longstreet, with two of his divisions went to Tennessee in an effort to aid General Braxton Bragg. At the same time, Meade also lost two of his corps, the 11th and 12[th,] when they were detached and sent toward Chattanooga.

By the end of September, Lee decided to go on the offensive and ordered his army to move eastward. In moving eastward toward Washington, Lee hoped to outflank Meade, but the Union commander was aware of Lee's movements. He also had his army on the move. Soon these two great armies clashed near Bristoe Station on October 14 and Ambrose P. Hill lost two of his experienced commanders, General's John R. Cooke and General William W. Kirland.

Lee immediately pulled his army back. Once more, the Army of Northern Virginia moved south of the Rappahannock. Doing so, Lee ordered the fortification of the crossings both at Rappahannock Station and at Kelly's Fords. In the meantime, Meade, wanting to move on Fredericksburg, was thwarted when his superiors ordered him instead to retake the area between the Rappahannock and the Rapidan. Once more, Meade advanced toward Culpeper, but as he neared Kelly's Ford, his army ran into the guards watching the crossings. Union forces were successful in crossing Kelly's Ford on the evening of November 7 despite a night assault ordered by Lee. Thwarted, Lee was forced to withdraw once more toward Orange Court House.

After these three short campaigns, five men from Company H of the 3d North Carolina Infantry Regiment were reported as having left camp on November 15 while the company was camped near Raccoon Ford. Two additional men, from the same company, were also reported to have deserted when they had left camp on November 25, 1863 as the regiment was encamped near Morton's Ford. These seven men belonged to the same company that witnessed the death of six of their comrades by firing squad two months previous. In essence, the executions did not stopped the desertion rate, it only made the men more careful in their actions and the routes they took to get home.

Five days before the execution of the ten North Carolinians, the New York Times, on August 31, 1863, reported five members of the Fifth Corps were to be executed for desertion after being denied a pardon by President Lincoln. The article also mentioned that there was thirty more awaiting trials and undoubtedly would also be given the same fate. In this article, the reporter commented that "their death is necessary to save hundreds of other lives, and to put a stop to the desertion of this class of men." Thus, desertions were common and universal for both armies. No matter how many were executed on either side, the desertion rate did not stop and execution was not the answer to the problem. Soldiers continued to leave camp, continued to walk away from their obligations and left their comrades and their honor behind.

During the time of this terrible conflict that tore this nation apart, there were over 268,530 desertions according to Fox's Regimental Losses (Chapter XIII, page 531). But this number was later revised to 201,397 as some of the stragglers, thought to be deserters, had returned to camp. Of this number, approximately 75,000 soldiers were captured, placed under arrest and punished in some manner. In the Union army alone, 267 men were executed by military court-martial of which 147 were for actual desertion. Figures for the Confederate army is non-existent due to many records being destroyed during and immediately after the war.

Fifty years after the outbreak of hostilities and forty-eight years after his death in Scottsville, Virginia, Richardson Mallett was finally awarded the degree he would have received had he stayed in school. In 1911, the University of North Carolina at Chapel Hill awarded degrees to all those students who had left the University to serve in the Confederacy. Mallett finally received his AB degree posthumously to 1862, the year he would have graduated. He, like many others, had left their education behind to join the young Confederacy and support their state by taking up arms against fellow Americans.

When this story was started, it was meant to be a story of two sets of brothers — the Futch's and the Mallett's, of which only one survived the war. As for the Futch brothers, Charley and John, neither survived: Charley died on Culp's Hill during the heat of battle on July 2, 1863 and his younger

103

brother, John, died September 5, 1863, shot to death by his own brigade. As for the Mallett brothers, one survived. Young Richardson Mallett died on August 25, 1863, shot as he attempted to effect the arrest of the deserters. His older brother, Colonel Charles Peter (Peter) Mallett, the commander of the North Carolina conscripts, survived until November 27, 1907 dying at the age of 82. Incidentally, Peter, indirectly, conscripted some of his younger brother's killers.

However, this story instead took on a meaning of its own as it told the story of a tragic event that occurred during that terrible war over a hundred forty years ago. The Civil War eventually did unite this country but only after it first tore it apart. The war had its heroes, its moments of valor, it moments of glory but it also had its tragic moments as brother fought against brother, father against son. Men died not only on the battlefield, but also of disease leaving behind countless widows and children, some of whom never knew their fathers. Many men were so badly injured, both physically and mentally, that they could no longer function in the world around them. It is impossible to describe what type of life they or their families endured after the war.

Most of the men who took up arms did their duty. They performed in an exceptional manner. They marched, they fought and they marched some more. They obeyed orders and did as they were told. They wanted nothing more than the war to end so they could go home to family and friends. There were a very small number of men though who did not do their duty for various reasons. Who knows why a soldier, in any war, decides to leave his comrades and his honor behind. This is one of the tragedies of war.

Unfortunately this tragic event occurred on the grounds of Montpelier, the former home of the fourth President of the United States. James Madison had a dream and a vision for a strong, powerful united nation and he worked all of his life toward that accomplishment. The dream was finally fulfilled, but only after a terrible war, that tested the boundaries, strengths and ideas of man. Eventually the war did result in a stronger and greater nation, one that now can be said to really be "indivisible and with liberty for all."

---

[1] Richard B. Harwell, *The Civil War Reader: The Consequence of Desertion,* (New York, Knoecky & Knoecky, 1958), p. 269.
[2] ibid.

Chapter Nine

Who Were They?

Exactly who was the young adjutant who lost his life while doing his duty? Who were the men who left their comrades, shot and killed the adjutant, disgraced their families and ultimately paid the supreme price for their actions? All of them had a life before this terrible tragedy. They had families and friends, feelings and emotions, and all at first had the greatest expectations of doing what was right and just. A tragic event occurred on the grounds of Montpelier that day in September. It serves today as a tragic reminder of some events that did occur during those four volatile years in our nation's history.

Though records of the ten men shot for desertion and murder have disappeared, the event is mentioned in diaries, newspapers, and in some books. References are made to the execution and, in some, it is mentioned that ten men were shot, but their names are not revealed. It is as if they ceased to exist on the day they were shot. Who were these ten men? Did they leave behind family or children to carry on their names?

After much searching, digging and patience, the below information is all that can be found, at this time, for the men involved. No birthdays could be located for any of the deserters, no pictures or photographs, and no family memories could be found. At times, it seems like these men never existed. Court records reveal very little as most records in North Carolina prior to 1913 have been destroyed. Letters of only one of the men were found. In the majority of the cases, no family or friends to claim them except this writer. They remain in an unmarked grave someplace on or near Montpelier Station, Virginia. They are lost to eternity.

Perhaps one day, their remains will be uncovered and to insure that their names and their existence are not lost or forgotten, I have enclose what little information I had been able to located. Their existence should be acknowledge for it shows what really did occur during the years that this nation was involved in a great struggle known as the Civil War.

1. <u>William Barefoot</u>, **executed** September 5, 1863 at the age of 29. Born in 1834 to John B. and Nancy (Register) Barefoot, residents of the township of Whiteville. William, a farmer by trade, enlisted in Company H, 3d North Carolina on February 15, 1862 in Columbus County, North Carolina. He was captured by Union forces during a skirmish at Boonsboro, Maryland on September 16, 1862, and confined at Fort Delaware until exchanged on October 2, 1862. He returned to duty with the 3rd North Carolina on January 30, 1863. Between those dates, he was reported to have been absent without leave, and is believed to have gone home to spend time with his family. He was married to Elizabeth Batton (listed as 22 years old on the 1860 census), and is believed to have fathered three children. (Only two are listed on the 1860 census (Martha, age 2 and Napoleon Bonaparte, age 1 month.). (1860 Federal Census North Carolina Database: ID #NC4457370, County of Columbus, Township of Whiteville, Page 955.)

2. <u>Francis Benson</u>, **executed** September 5, 1863 at the age of 26. Enlisted from Bladen County in Company H, 3d North Carolina on May 18, 1861. Known as Frank, he was reported as being sick at home from March 14, 1862 to October 31, 1862 according to the Confederate Reports.

Records in Bladen County Courthouse, located in Elizabethtown, indicated that a Francis Benson was married to Margaret Daniels and one child was born of that marriage. It is unknown at this time if this is the same man that was executed in 1863. Another entry was located for Francis Benson indicating he was killed at Gettysburg. In checking the Confederate Death Roster for Gettysburg, the name of Frank or Francis Benson does not appear. It was common practice to list men who died months after the Battle of Gettysburg to have been a casualty of that battle if it was known that they had been there. The same record that indicates he was killed at Gettysburg also indicates he was married to Jane Sprague. A daughter, Cornelia, was born of that marriage in late 1862. This baby died six months later.

3. <u>John R. Bedsole,</u> **executed** September 5, 1863. Not much had been found on Bedsole. Records indicate he enlisted in Company H, 3d North Carolina on February 15, 1862 from Columbus County and was wounded at Malvern Hill on July 1, 1862. Two months later, on September 17, 1862, he was promoted to full corporal. The next entry on his service record indicates he deserted on August 20, 1863. No further records could be located on him or any possible family relations. He does not appear on any of the 1860 census records for North Carolina.

4. <u>James D. Bunn,</u> **executed** September 5, 1863 at the age of 20. According to Confederate Records, there were two Bunn's in Company K, 3rd North Carolina Infantry Regiment: Dallas Bunn and James D. Bunn. Records for both are identical with each giving the age at the time of enlistment as 19, showing that both resided in Wake County. Both were conscripted on July 15, 1862 and both

were listed as being "absent." A note next to that shows that both were "sent to the rear from Orange C.H." on 8/27/1862. This note remains on both records until February 28, 1863 when it shows both of them to be present with the company. Both records also reflect they were captured on May 3 1863 during the Battle of Chancellsorville and paroled the following day. The final entry on each record indicates they were present and accounted for until the muster rolls of August 31, 1863 when both are listed as having deserted. A notation for each shows they "carried ordnance to the amount of $33.98." Both records also indicate that both were executed on September 5, 1863.

If this is the case, then there would have been eleven men shot that day and all official records and newspapers account indicate only ten men went to their death that day. In all probability, there was only one Bunn and his name was James Dallas Bunn. Newspapers accounts of the time do not complete clarify the issue, only confuse it more. The newspaper accounts list only ten names and three of those names are Bunn: Francis, Dorsey, and a B. Bunn, all assigned to Company H. Official records for Company H indicates there were no Bunns' in the company but there were four Bunn's assigned to Company K: the two listed above and a George A. and Wesley Bunn. George was captured by Union forces on October 19, 1864 and remained until exchanged on March 17, 1865. Wesley was also captured by Union forces on September 17, 1862 and "requested not to be exchange and was permitted to proceed to and remain in any of the loyal states."

It is ironic that the records indicate that Bunn was conscripted by Major Peter Mallett who was the brother of the adjutant that Bunn, with the other deserters, were accused of killing on August 25, 1863 near Scottsville, Virginia. No records could be located on any family information on any of the Bunns' listed above.

5. Duncan R. Clarke, **executed** September 5, 1863 at the age of 21. He enlisted in Company H, 3d North Carolina on May 15, 1861 from Bladen County, North Carolina and was wounded during the Battle of Chancellsorville on May 3, 1863. No other family records could be located for him.

6. James T. Ellis, **executed** on September 5, 1863 at the age of 33. He enlisted in Company H, 3d North Carolina on February 10, 1862 from Columbus County. He was wounded during the Battle of Sharpsburg [Antietam] on September 17, 1862 and apparently the wound was minor as he quickly returned to his company. According to records in the Columbus County Court House, located in Whiteville, North Carolina, he was married to Eleanor Powers on May 11, 1854. Since he and William Barefoot were both from Whiteville, in all probability, they were friends and comrades. No children or other relatives could be located for Ellis. (Deed of Registrar for Whiteville, Columbus County Court House and appears on the 1860 federal Census North Carolina Database ID #NC44548558 County of Columbus, Town of Whiteville, page 992.)

7. Hanson M. Futch, **died of Smallpox** on December 18, 1863 at the age of 21 Enlisted in Company K, 3d North Carolina on June 1, 1861 from New Hanover County. He had been wounded at Scottsville, Virginia while resisting arrest and had been remanded to Castle Thunder under sentence of death. He was the son of Jacob Futch of Holly Shelter Township and came from a rather large family.

111

According to the 1860 Census, Hanson had one older sister and six younger brothers. His death from smallpox was announced in the Wilmington Daily Journal of January 7, 1864. The 1870 Census for the Futch's of Holly Shelter Township listed another boy, born in 1864, named Hanson. It is believed this boy was named for his older brother – whether as a remembrance to him or to completely obliterate any existence of the son that had deserted in a time of war. (Marriage & Death Notices -- Wilmington newspapers, page 75, item 724] (Daily Journal January 7, 1864 /weekly journal of January 14, 1864.] compiled & indexed by Helen Moore Sammons, 1987 copied at the New Hanover County Public Library, 201 Chestnut, Wilmington, NC], and 1860 and 1870 Federal Census for New Hanover, North Carolina, Township of Holly Shelter.)

8. <u>John Thomas Futch,</u> **executed** on September 5, 1863 at the age of 27. He had enlisted in Company K, 3d North Carolina from Harnett County though he was a resident of Topsail Sound in New Hanover County. It is believed he did so to be near an older brother. He married Martha Ramsey on February 11, 1862. According to his service record, he was listed as being sick from April 15, 1862 to February 28, 1863 with a notation that he had returned home to recover. On his service record, it is indicated that he was one who had taken his rifle with him when he deserted. The notation states he "carried with him ordnance to the amount of $33.98." After his death, John's wife, with his son from a previous marriage to a woman by the name of Catherine, moved back to the home of her father, Martin Ramsey. In a previous marriage, John had 2 children, Charles, age 3 and John Thomas. This is reflected on the 1860 census for New Hanover County, Township of Topsail Sound. What happened to Catherine and Charles is unknown. (1860 Census Rolls For New

Hanover County, Township of Topsoil Sound, Page 170; 1870 Census Rolls for New Hanover County, Township of Topsoil Sound; Marriage and Death Notices from Wilmington Newspapers, page 75, item 725. (Daily Journal February 26, 1862 and Weekly Journal February 27, 1862, compiled and indexed by Helen Moore Sammons, 1987 copied at the New Hanover County Public Library, 201 Chestnut, Wilmington, NC.)

9. <u>William H. Kelly</u>, **executed** on September 5, 1863 at the age of 22. He had enlisted in Company H, 3d North Carolina on June 24, 1861 from Bladen County. Not much is known of him except what is listed in the 1860 census. William appears to have been the youngest child of William and M.J. Kelley. His father is listed as a farmer and an older brother appears to have been a cooper [barrel maker].

10. <u>Richardson Mallett,</u> **shot to death effecting the arrest of the deserters** on August 25, 1863 near Scottsville, Virginia. Richardson was born in Fayettville, North Carolina on September 12, 1840 and was the first born son of Sarah Green Mallett, the second wife of Charles Peter Mallett. Richardson's father had six children born to his first wife, Sophia Sarah Beatty. Sophia died on February 20, 1829. Ten years later, Charles Mallett took Sarah as his second wife.

Richardson was a student of the University of North Carolina at Chapel Hill where his courses were strong in mathematics, languages and religion. Upon the outbreak of the Civil War, Richardson left school after his junior year and joined the 46th North Carolina. According to an article that appeared in the Southern Historical Papers, in 1898, "The residents of the village of Chapel Hill were among the earliest to enter the service. They had their representatives at Bethel. A company was organized early in April. Among its officers were R. J. Ashe, as captain; R.B. Saunders and R. Mallett, as second lieutenants, and Thomas G. Skinner, as fourth corporal. It will thus be seen that the company was under the direction of University Men. "

Richardson's older brother, Peter, had formed Company C of the 3d North Carolina and in 1862 was placed in charge of conscripts for the State of North Carolina. Another older brother, Edward Jones, had joined the 61st North Carolina and was killed during one of the last battles of the Civil War, the battle of Bentonville on March 22,1865. In 1911, Richardson was finally awarded his AB degree dating to 1862, the year he was to graduate. The University also indicates that Richardson was killed at Gettysburg as does the article in the Southern Historical Papers. (The Southern Historical Society Papers, Vol. XXIV, 1896, Page 12, CD-ROM, Guild press of Indiana, Inc., Carmel, In., and General Alumni Association, Alumni History of the University of North Carolina, 2d edition, Durham, NC Christian and King Printing Co., 1924 (copied at the University of North Carolina at Chapel Hill, Chapel Hill, North Carolina)

10. Kearney Privett, **executed** on September 5, 1863 at the age of 20. He had enlisted in Company K, 3d North Carolina from Wake County. He is believed to have come from the town of Earpsborough. According to his service record, he was taken prisoner during the Battle of Sharpsburg (Antietam) on September 17, 1862 and was paroled November 10, 1862 and returned to his company. No other information could be located on Privett. (1860 Federal Census North Carolina Database #ID NC44513 page 438.)

11. <u>John N. Rainer</u>, **executed** on September 5, 1863 at the age of 20. He enlisted in Company K, 3d North Carolina from New Hanover County on June 1, 1861. Wounded during the Battle of Malvern Hill on July 1, 1862, Rainer returned to active duty January 17, 1863. No other information could be located for him.

12. <u>William R. Stell</u>, age 29, is **believed to have been killed resisting arrest** near Scottsville, Virginia on August 25, 1863. He was married on October 30, 1860 to Eliza A. Watkins. He enlisted in Company K, 3d North Carolina on July 15, 1862 from Wake County. His service records at first list him as being sick and he is then reported to having deserted on August 11 with other members of Company K. The last entry of his service record was on August 11, 1863. It is believed he left with the other men who were captured near Scottsville. Since all reference to him stops on that date and it had been mentioned that several of the deserters were killed in the exchange of gunfire, it is strongly believe that he was one of the men killed that day. He does have related family members today still residing in North Carolina but information of him is very sketchy.

13. <u>James A. Tuter</u>, is **believed to have been killed resisting arrest** near Scottsville, Virginia on August 25, 1863. Tutor enlisted in Company K, 3d North Carolina on July 15, 1862 from Harnett County. He is reported to have deserted on August 11, the same day as other members of Company K were to have left. It is believed he was one of those killed in Scottsville as no other records exist of him from August 11, 1863.

Bibliography

Published Sources:

Axelrod, Alan. *The Complete Idiot's Guide to the Civil War*. New York: Alpha Books, division of MacMillan Reference, 1998.

Bates, Samuel P. *Battle of Gettysburg*. Philadelphia:n.p.,1875.

Brandy, Ken., *The Gettysburg Papers*., 2 Volumes (Reissued in One Volume). Dayton, Ohio: Morningside Press, 1986.

Busby, John W. and David G. Martin. *Regimental Strengths and Losses at Gettysburg*. New York: Longstreet House, 1994.

Casler, John O. *Four Years In The Stonewall Brigade*. Dayton, Ohio: Morningside Press, 1971.

Clark, Champ, and the Editors of Time-Life Books. *Gettysburg: The Confederate High Tide*, New York: Time-Life Books, 1985.

Davis, William C., *Confederate General (6Volumes)*. National Historical Society, 1991.

Doubleday, Abner. *Chancellorsville and Gettysburg*. New York: Da Capo Press, 1994.

Garrison, Webb. *The Encyclopedia of Civil War Usage*., Nashville, Tenn.: Cumberland House, 2001.

Gettysburg Death Roster: The Confederate Dead at Gettysburg. Compiled by Robert K. Krick. Dayton, Ohio: Morningside Press, 1993.

Goldsborough, W.W. *The Maryland Line in the Confederate Army*. Baltimore: n.p., 1990.

Harwell, Richard B. *The Civil War Reader: The Consequence of Desertion*. New York: Knoecky & Knoecky, 1958.

Howard, McHenry. *Recollections of a Maryland Confederate Soldier and Staff Officer under Johnston, Jackson and Lee*. Dayton, Ohio: Morningside Press, 1975.

Hurst, Patricia J. *Soldiers, Stories, Sites and Fights: Orange County, Virginia 1861-1865*, Rapidan, Virginia: Patricia J. Hurst, 1998.

Johnson, Robert Underwood, and Buel, Clarence Clough, eds. *Battles and Leaders of the Civil War*, 4 volumes, reprint edition. Secaucus, New Jersey. Castle.

Ketcham, Ralph. *James Madison: A Biography.* Charlottesville, Virginia: University Press of Virginia, 1990.

Ladd, David L. and Audrey J. Ladd. *The Bachelder Papers: Gettysburg In Their Own Words.*, 3 volumes, Dayton, Ohio: Morningside Press, 1994.

Long, E.B. with Barbara Long. *The Civil War: Day By Day, An Almanac 1861 – 1865.* (Reprint of Doubleday & Co.) New York: DaCapo Press, 1971.

McKim, Randolph. *A Soldier's Recollections.* New York: Longman's Green, and Co., 1910.

Meade, George G. *The Life and Letters of George G. Meade: Gettysburg,* (Reprint). York, Pennsylvania: Graphic Works, 1998.

——— *The Life and Letters of George G. Meade.* New York: Charles Scribner's Sons, 1913.

New York Monuments Commission for the Battlefields of Gettysburg. Final Report on the Battlefield at Gettyburg, 3 volumes. Albany, New York: J.B. Lyon Company, 1900.

North Carolina Troops 1861-65, A Roster, Compiled by Weymouth T. Jordan Jr., Vol. XI. Raleigh, North Carolina: Division of Archives and History, 1987.

——— A Roster, Compiled by Louis H. Manarin, Vol. III. Raleigh, North Carolina: State Department of Archives and History, 1971.

Rakove, Jack N., ed. *Madison: Writings.* New York: Library of America, 1999.

Rutland, Robert A. ed., *James Madison and the American Nation 1751-1836: An Encyclopedia.* New York: Simon and Schulster, New York, 1994.

United States War Department. *The War of the Rebellion: A Compilation of the Official Records of the Union and Confederate Armies*, 128 volumes. Washington, DC: Government Printing Office, 1880-1901.

Virginia Regimental History Series, Lynchburg, Va. H.E. Howard, Inc., 1987.

Warner, Ezra J. *Generals In Blue.* Baton Rouge, Louisiana: Louisiana State University   Press, 1964.

———— *Generals In Gray.* Baton Rouge, Louisiana: Louisiana State University Press, 1959.

Articles and Manuscripts:

Elmore, Thomas L. "Courage Against the Trenches: The Attack and Repulse of Steuart's Brigade on Culp's Hill." *Gettysburg Magazine*, Vol. 7.

Emerson, A.J. "A Boy in the Camp of Lee." *Confederate Veteran Magazine*, Vol. 24, 1916.

General Alumni Association, *Alumni History of the University of North Carolina*, 2d edition. Durham, North Carolina: Christian and King Printing Co., 1924.

Hall, Clark B., "Seasons of Change: Winter Encampment of the Army of the Potomac December 1, 1863 - May 4, 1864." *Blue and Gray Magazine*, March 16, 1991.

Jorgensen, Jay., "Joseph W. Latimer, The Boy Major at Gettysburg."*Gettysburg Magazine*, Vol. 10.

———— "Holding the Right: The 137th New York Regiment at Gettysburg.", *Gettysburg Magazine*, Vol. 15.

Weeks, Stephen B., ed., *Biographical Sketches of the Confederate Dead of the University of North Carolina,* North Carolina University Magazine, New Series, IX., No. 2.

CD-ROM and Internet Sites:

Civil War Prisons: Castle Thunder (1999)
    <http://www.mdgorman.com/castle_thunder.htm>
Confederate Military History. [CD-ROM]. Carmel, Indiana:
    Guild Press of Indiana,
Fox, William F. Regimental Losses in the American Civil War
    1861-1865. (CD-ROM). Carmel, Indiana: Guild Press
    of Indiana.
Genealogy Site: <http://www.Ancestry.com>
Southern Historical Papers (52 Volumes). [CD-ROM].
    Carmel, Indiana: Guild Press of Indiana.

Other Sources:

Compiled Service Records of Confederate Service Records
    Who Served in Organization from North Carolina
    Rolls [RG109] Microfilm ID M270 (Rolls 123 -131),
    National Archives, Washington, DC.
Cumberland County Survey, Fayetteville Genealogy Society,
    Vol. 1, Fayetteville, North Carolina.
Deed of Registrar, Columbus County Court House,
    Whiteville, North Carolina.
Deed of Registrar, Orange County Court House, Orange,
    Virginia.
Futch Letters, July-August, 1863, Private Collections (PC.507
    – 3B), Courtesy of the North Carolina Office of
    Archives and History, Division of Historical
    Resources, Raleigh, North Carolina.
Justice, Benjamin Wesley, Letter to his wife dated September
    7, 1863, Courtesy of the Montpelier Archives,
    Montpelier Station, Virginia.
Kearns, Watkins, Diary: May 17, 1863 -February 29, 1864,
    MSS 5:1 K2143:3 Courtesy of the Virginia Historical
    Society, Richmond, Virginia.
Mallett Genealogy Page, http://www. Ancestry.Com.

Marriages & Death Notices – Wilmington newsapapers,
    Compiled and indexed by Helen Moore Sammons,
    New Hanover County Library, Wilmington, North
    Carolina.
Miller, Ann, Structural Report of Montpelier, copied at
    Montpelier, Montpelier Station, Virginia.
Schlotterbeck, John T. Civil War: The Confederate Frontier:
    Orange and Green Counties, Paper presented at the
    Southern Historical Associates Meeting in Charleston,
    SC on November 12, 1983.
Steuart, George H. Papers, Courtesy of the Eleanor S.
    Brockenbrough Library, Museum of the Confederacy,
    Richmond, Virginia.
University Student Records, Scholarship 1852 – 1866, v. 3,
    Wilson Library, University of North Carolina at
    Chapel Hill, Chapel Hill, North Carolina.

Drawings copied from the Dover Clip Art Series, *Authentic
    Civil War Illustrations*, Selected and Arranged by
    Carol Belanger Grafton, Dover Publications Inc.,
    New York 1995

"I would like to come home. But I do not know
when I will get the chance to come again. But I
am going to come before long if I have to runnaway
to do it"

John Futch, July 31, 1863